Reclaiming
the Ground

Reclaiming the Ground

The Biblical Basis and Practice of Breaking Curses on Land and Cleansing Buildings from Evil Spirits

Ken Hepworth

Sovereign World

Sovereign World Ltd
PO Box 784
Ellel
Lancaster LA1 9DA
England
www.sovereignworld.com

ISBN 978 1 85240 499 4

Cover design by Andrew Mark, ThirteenFour Design
Typeset by CRB Associates, Reepham, Norfolk
Printed in Malta

Contents

Acknowledgements

"When are you going to write a book Ken?" has been said to me on numerous occasions. My reply has always been "When the Lord gives me something to write about"! Well with this book I have found something to write about. I am deeply indebted to several people who have encouraged me to write on the issues surrounding the subject matter of this book, such as David Noakes with whom I first discussed the idea (after my wife), and who has been kind enough to make suggestions following the reading of my manuscript. Others who read the manuscript and gave invaluable comments as well as the encouragement to write this book are, Joan Thomas, James Burn, Pennant and Maureen Jones, and Lissa Smith. Lissa's expertise has been an enormous help to me in the many editorial suggestions she has made. Her smiley faces, drawn alongside grammatical and obscure points, made it easy for me to make the necessary corrections.

I am also indebted to my family who have encouraged me. Especially my youngest son David, who is now a member of the preaching team in his local church and has been brave enough to share with his dad some of the weaknesses he found in the manuscript. Most acknowledgements make mention of a spouse who has had to put up with hours of solitude whilst their partner worked long hours on the book. My wife Jean is no exception to this, and I am deeply grateful to her for her advice, encouragement and patience.

No book is perfect and in offering this to you the reader I am aware of this fact. I alone am responsible for its final content. However, I wish to acknowledge that I was first introduced to the concept of Reclaiming the Ground from the teaching of Peter Horrobin, the founder and International Director of Ellel Ministries International. Under his leadership in recent years, I have enjoyed the privilege of serving the Lord in the proclamation of the kingdom of God, through evangelism, healing and deliverance.

Finally, I wish to thank Tim Pettingale from Sovereign World for his helpful suggestions and for the willingness of Sovereign World to publish this book. My prayer is that this book will be a help to Christian leaders everywhere, and especially to pastors of local churches, who are called by Jesus Christ to destroy the devil's works.

Introduction

Why is it that some churches experience blessings through increased membership and spiritual growth in their members whilst others struggle to maintain their very existence? Why is it that some churches that were on the cutting edge of what God was doing are now in decline? Why are some churches never able to move away from the past with its empty traditions that are stifling the life of the church? One important and often unrecognized factor lies in the spiritual forces operating over the buildings, land and corporate organizations.

There are three main areas of attack from the powers of darkness. The first is through the foothold that evil spirits may have in the personal lives of believers. This book assumes an understanding of the deliverance ministry. If you do not believe that Christians can be demonized then may I suggest that you read the book on deliverance from evil spirits by Peter Horrobin.[1] Scripture says that we can give the devil a foothold in our life through sin (Ephesians 4:27). Demons are unlikely to go away quietly because we sing songs such as: "Satan has no authority here", however heartily we may sing them. We must confess and repent of our sins, but we must also deal with the consequences of our sins, especially where these consequences have opened individuals as well as the life of the Fellowship to the presence of unclean spirits.

Secondly, the apostle Paul says, *"for our struggle is ... against the spiritual forces of evil in the heavenly realms"* (Ephesians 6:12). This is a reference to the powers of the air. If Scripture says that

---

[1] *Healing Through Deliverance* published by Sovereign World, 2008.

I have spiritual opponents who seek to wrestle with me in order to stop me doing God's will, then I need to learn how to identify their tactics and overcome their purposes (2 Corinthians 2:11)!

Thirdly, and this is the main subject matter of this book, demonic powers can be present in our buildings because they have been given access either to the land that the church is built upon or to the corporate structure and life of the church itself. From this vantage point demons can influence individual believers and thus undermine the life of the whole church or fellowship. They are able in most instances to do this without encountering any resistance even from the leadership of the church. They can do so because they are spiritual beings, which are invisible to the human eye. To detect their presence and operation requires spiritual understanding and the exercise of spiritual discernment. It is my hope that this book will provide a biblical basis for understanding deliverance, which will drive us to prayer, resulting in action directed by the Holy Spirit.

My plea is that those who read this book search and read each scripture reference quoted in order to verify the accuracy of the teaching.

Chapter 1

Satan's Present Dominion and Authority

Before looking at the issue of how demons gain and use access to land and buildings, I want to lay a biblical foundation concerning the authority and power that Satan and his demons are able to exercise in this age.

This present age

The Bible describes the age in which we currently live as "this present evil age" (Galatians 1:4). History has not yet reached the point when through Christ, the Day of the Lord will surely come and Satan's reign of death and destruction will come to a shameful end for him (2 Peter 3:10; 1 John 3:8; Acts 10:38; Revelation 20:7–10). Until that time, Satan continues to have a domain and the power to rule over it. His kingdom is described as "the dominion of darkness" (Colossians 1:13; Acts 26:18). Jesus Christ Himself described Satan as the prince of this world (John 12:31; 14:30; 16:11).

The Bible also identifies other fallen spiritual beings that are under Satan's control and that assist him in his wicked plans and purposes (Matthew 25:41; Revelation 12:7) and who, with him, exercise the present rule of darkness (Ephesians 6:12). They exercise this rule over and through men and women who are under Satan's control and together with them they are described as the rulers of this age (1 John 5:19; 2 Corinthians 4:4; Ezekiel 28:1–19; 1 Corinthians 2:8). Their power will eventually be crushed and they will all be cast into the Lake of Fire (1 Corinthians 15:24–26; Revelation 19:20 and 20:10–15), but at this present time they are able to resist and sometimes even attack the children of God in their pursuit against the will of God.

Satan will do everything he can to try and prevent mankind from receiving salvation; however his work does not stop when someone comes to faith in Christ. Many Christians can testify that their problems began in earnest after having made their decision to follow Christ. Satan cannot stop the kingdom of God coming in its fullness (Daniel 2:44), but Christian history supports the fact that he can hinder and oppose the work of God. An example of this hindering can be seen in the ministry of the apostle Paul. He wanted to visit the Thessalonians but Satan was able to stop him and those with him (1 Thessalonians 2:18). The Bible doesn't say how Satan did this.

Sometimes, the attack against Christians is much more serious than a mere hindrance. The powers of darkness can directly attack the child of God (James 4:7; 1 Peter 5:8; 1 Corinthians 15:32) and their attack is often carried out through the people in this world who do not belong to Christ (Revelation 2:10). It is even possible for Christians to provide the enemy with such an opportunity. The acts of the sinful nature as outlined in Galatians 5:19–21 can be described as the devil's workshop. Through the practice of these sins in our lives, demonic powers can forge weapons of attack against our fellow believers. Only Jesus could say that He was entirely free from any hold that Satan might use:

> *"I will not speak much more with you, for the ruler of the world is coming, and he has nothing in Me."*
>
> (John 14:30 NASB)

On one occasion Paul was stoned, although it is not clear from Scripture how seriously he was injured. It is likely, however, that the believers who surrounded him prayed for him, as he was able to carry on with his journey the very next day (Acts 14:19–20). Sadly, believers may be injured or lose their lives as a result of such attacks, for example in road accidents. Although Satan may not be involved in every such incident we have nevertheless ministered to accident victims for whom this was undoubtedly the truth.

Jesus is Lord over all

God the Father has already placed all rule and authority, whether human or spiritual, under the supreme authority of His Son Jesus Christ (Matthew 28:18; Ephesians 1:20–23; Colossians 1:16–18; 1 Corinthians 15:24). History is moving towards a complete expression of this inescapable fact, when the Son of God will bring everything under submission to His will and then hand over a redeemed creation to God the Father (1 Corinthians 15:24–28). Although we do not, in this present age, see Christ's rule fully established, Scripture declares that He must reign until He has put all His enemies under His feet (1 Corinthians 15:25). The day is coming when:

> *"It is written: 'as surely as I live,' says the Lord, 'every knee will bow before me; every tongue will confess to God.'"*
>
> (Romans 14:11)

This future reign of Christ will extend from the time of His return over the whole earth during the period of His millennial kingdom (Matthew 13:31–32; Luke 7:21; Habakkuk 2:14). During this time Satan (and presumably all demons), will be bound in the abyss for a thousand years (Revelation 20:1–4). Following this time Satan will be loosed for a little time before being finally destroyed. This will in turn lead to God's creation of a new heaven and a new earth, in which neither Satan, sin, darkness nor even disease will be present (Revelation 21:1–5).

Satan's present power base

At this present time however, Satan clearly has a power base from which he can operate, despite the fact that Jesus Christ has already won the victory over him (Revelation 2:13, 13:2 and 16:10). Does that victory mean that Christian disciples can proclaim the kingdom of God without having to do battle against the enemy? The New Testament offers no basis on which to substantiate this false idea (1 Timothy 1:18; 6:12). The Lord has commissioned us to enforce the victory through spiritual warfare as His co-workers, acting with His authority.

There is a fight to be fought

It has been said that for evil to triumph all that is needed is for good men to do nothing. Many Christians today seem to think that since Jesus has died and risen again, the powers of darkness are not a problem that they have to deal with. If this is so, why does Scripture give us such warnings as found in 1 Peter 5:8–9:

> *"Be self-controlled and alert. Your enemy the devil prowls around like a roaring lion looking for someone to devour. Resist him, standing firm in the faith, because you know that your brothers throughout the world are undergoing the same kind of sufferings."*

We are called to be active in our stand against evil (Luke 9:1–2; 10:17; Ephesians 6:16–18; Romans 12:21; 2 Corinthians 2:11). This includes the casting out of demons (Matthew 10:8; Luke 9:1–6; 10:17–20). We must not be ignorant of the schemes of Satan otherwise he will outwit us. Time and again Scripture encourages us to fight and to stand our ground (1 Timothy 6:12; Ephesians 6:14). We are not to expect the Lord to fight this battle without our participation. However, neither must we engage in this fight without an adequate understanding of the exact nature of the battle. We need to know the enemy's strengths and tactics and what weapons we should use to defeat him. If we do not give time to learning about these issues then our fighting will be ineffective (1 Corinthians 9:26; 14:8) and we shall become casualties of war, whether we are active or passive. Many civilians or non-combatants were killed in the last two world wars. There are many casualties among Christians today. Pastors leave the ministry for various reasons. Churches are closing in every city, town and village. People are leaving the Church because of relationships that break down, or because they don't have the inner strength to sustain Christian discipleship. These are clear examples of the success of Satan's tactics, but all too often the Church fails to see them for what they really are.

Understanding the authority of Satan

How can Satan do what he does? What is it that gives him the right to cause so much damage to the Church? We need to consider the rights that are given to Satan through sin, for unless we understand how the enemy gains access, we shall not have either the knowledge or the power to remove him. Let us ask an important question: how did Satan become the prince of this world? (John 12:31; 14:30; 16:11).

The consequence of Adam's sin

To understand the enormous consequences of the sin of our first parents (Genesis 3:4–6; Romans 5:12) we need to examine particularly the second temptation that Satan offered Jesus in the wilderness:

> *"The devil led him up to a high place and showed him in an instant all the kingdoms of the world. And he said to him, 'I will give you all their authority and splendour, for it has been given to me, and I can give it to anyone I want to. So if you worship me, it will all be yours.'"*   (Luke 4:5–7)

Satan said that the kingdoms of this world had been given to him. Is this true or false? If false, then why did Jesus not correct him? The reason He did not do so is because what Satan said is true. Let us then ask the question, "Who gave it to Satan?" The answer is that our first parents did, for it was through their sin that Satan gained access to dominate the world. Before they sinned, Adam and Eve had dominion (Genesis 1:28), but when they sinned they lost the moral right and also the spiritual authority to govern the creation. Spiritual authority comes from God who gives it to those He chooses in order to accomplish His will and purposes. It was no longer possible to exercise this authority once rebellion had broken the relationship with the One who gave it – this was the terrible result of our first parents' sin in the Garden of Eden.

This world is now under the control of the evil one

Through their sin Adam and Eve came under the authority of Satan. Sin has given Satan an entrance into the world. This is why Scripture says in 1 John 5:19:

> *"We know that we are children of God, and that the whole world is under the control of the evil one."*

No Old Testament saint ever personally exercised authority over a demon to cast it out. It was not until Jesus came that a man, described in Scripture as the last Adam, i.e. the second or replacement Adam, had authority over Satan (1 Corinthians 15:45). Jesus demonstrated this authority when He healed a man who was blind and mute (Matthew 12:22–29). Jesus said,

> *"But if I drive out demons by the Spirit of God, then the kingdom of God has come upon you."*   (Matthew 12:28)

The physical problems that this man was experiencing were caused by the presence of demons. In order to heal him of his blindness and dumbness, Jesus had to cast the demons out. Demons can attack a person both from within or from without. The simple rule is that if they are on the outside, keep them out; if they are on the inside, cast them out. Jesus first demonstrated this authority and power in the synagogue in Capernaum (Mark 1:21–27). This incident occurred at the beginning of His ministry. The people were amazed at the authority Jesus demonstrated. To understand their amazement we need to understand that they had never seen this happen before. Not until Jesus came had a demon been dealt with in this way. Scripture teaches plainly now that Jesus has given to us His authority and power to cast out demons (Luke 10:17–18), and He expects us to use it! Not every person has this authority and power, but only believers in Jesus, whose names are written in heaven. The New Testament records the activities of some Jewish exorcists who discovered this fact in a painful way (Acts 19:13–20). During the last sixteen years of ministering to the sick and those in bondage, we have gained much understanding of the workings of the demonic realm.

Experience has taught us that usually demons do not go until they lose their legal right to be in residence, and are ordered to leave by Christian believers.

Deliverance from evil is not automatic

It is often assumed that when someone is born again, any demons present in the person have to leave. However uncomfortable the thought may be, this is not true, as many who have received personal ministry will testify! Some demons may go at conversion, and that is the testimony of a few. However, it would be wrong to assume that all demons have left or that any have left! To accept this fact does not undermine the work of the cross or in any way make it insufficient. Through the cross, Jesus has done all that is necessary to accomplish our eternal salvation, and we can add nothing to it nor can we take anything from it. However, if we are to experience the fullness of its power, we have to appropriate or take hold of it for ourselves personally and apply this finished work of Christ to our lives and our circumstances. Although Jesus has done all that is necessary to accomplish our salvation, there is something for us to do if what He has done is to become real in every area of our personal lives.

The story of the Passover illustrates this principle (Exodus 12). The lamb had been sacrificially slaughtered and its blood had been collected in a basin (Exodus 12:21–22). However, the blood was of no value to an Israelite until it was applied to the top and side of the doorframe of his dwelling (Exodus 12:22–23). Imagine what would have happened to the Israelite who did not follow the instructions to apply the lamb's blood to his doorframe. He would have experienced the death of his firstborn and livestock. Satan has been able to undermine the believer and the Church effectively for centuries without anyone discerning his presence or dealing with his power. Sadly, believers have had to live with the consequences of this lack of awareness, which has often meant sickness, sadness or even suicide for some.

However, we can apply the work of the cross by the Holy Spirit as we walk in obedience to Christ, proclaiming the gospel and praying specifically into situations where darkness is reigning and where we wish to establish the Lordship of Jesus. First, we need to know how the enemy is operating and how to take away his rights by discerning what gave him access in the first place and then removing his right to be there.

The extent of our authority

It is important that we do not exceed our God-given authority; otherwise we can make ourselves vulnerable to attack from evil spirits. For example, we have no authority to send the demons to the pit. Neither does Scripture give us authority to send demonic ruling spirits out of our town or city. We can, however, render their influence over Christian disciples and churches ineffective through personal deliverance and spiritual warfare for those who are willing to walk in obedience to Christ. For when we are in obedience to Christ we can expect to *"overcome all the power of the enemy"* in our own lives and in our spheres of influence and authority (Luke 10:19). That must include every demonic power because they are all under Satan's authority. If we have power over him, then we must have power over the whole of his domain. Please do not think that I am encouraging a casual approach to the enemy, in fact just the opposite. We are only effective against the devil's power when we are in right relationship with Christ and also when we are following His direction through the Holy Spirit. He alone can choose the issues, lead us against the foe, and decide the battleground.

Spiritual protection

In this fight against the powers of darkness the Lord has provided for us both spiritual weapons (2 Corinthians 10:4) and spiritual protection as outlined in Ephesians 6:10–18. We need not, in fact we must not, fear the power of the enemy, but neither must we assume that this protection is automatic. The clear requirement is that we know and practice the truth (Ephesians 6:14). Only Jesus could say that Satan had no hold on Him (John 14:30), but who of us can say this? Jesus was without any sin, but sadly we are not yet in the same position. We often choose to disobey the truth, without realizing that we are thereby making ourselves vulnerable to giving a demon a foothold in our life (Ephesians 4:27). Sometimes we are led into darkness through being deceived (2 Corinthians 11:13–14). Sin still gives Satan an opening today, so it is essential that we ask ourselves, does Satan have any opening in my life?

Jesus described personal deliverance from evil spirits as, *"... the children's bread ... "* (Matthew 15:26). A foreign woman was asking for deliverance from a demon that was causing terrible suffering to her daughter (Matthew 15:21–28). Who are the children that Jesus referred to? They are the covenant people of God. Salvation is first to the Jew and then to the Gentile (Romans 1:16). What is the significance of bread? Jesus described Himself as, *"the bread of life"* (John 6:35). It is also a basic dietary staple. It is not only general salvation that is in view here, but specifically deliverance from evil, which is inherent within God's plan of salvation (Matthew 6:13). So deliverance from evil spirits is primarily for those who receive salvation and are described as the children of God. Hence the comments of Jesus to this woman that it is not right to take what belongs to the children and give it to others. Jesus did, of course, respond to her great faith and granted her request. It is likely that His purpose in stating this truth, which at first sight would appear very discouraging to a Gentile woman, was actually calculated to draw out the response of faith which He recognized she possessed.

Chapter 2

The Battle for Holy Ground – Some Commonly Encountered Problems

The spiritual atmosphere

Spiritual darkness, resulting from the presence of evil spirits, will negatively affect the atmosphere and also hinder the activity of the Spirit of God in a building. Homeowners and, in particular, church leaders need to deal with the problem through removing the evil presence in order to change the spiritual atmosphere. The following chapters will give some examples and examine the scriptural basis for cleansing and delivering land, buildings and churches from visitation by evil spirits, and will explain the necessary procedures.

The spirit of Sikhism

Some years ago I led a church weekend on the subject of healing and deliverance in a Methodist Church in Bedford. On arrival the team began to pray around the church building, as is our normal custom. The object of doing this is to invite the presence of the Lord and to discern the presence of any spiritual darkness that needs dealing with by specific prayer, because if left unattended it could undermine the teaching and ministry, particularly on the subject of healing and deliverance. The team told me that they sensed real spiritual darkness down one side of the building. At this point, they did not know that the building next door to the church was being used as a Sikh temple. After I had shared this information, we took authority together over the spirit of Sikhism and bound its power in the name of Jesus Christ, forbidding it to interfere with our weekend. We asked the Lord to place His angels between us and the building next door. We also asked God to bless the Sikhs in the name of Jesus with the salvation that comes only through Him, for we wished them no harm. Following our prayer, the weekend of teaching and ministry was well received by the church.

The spirit of strife

Let me now give an example in relation to the presence of the enemy in our own homes. My wife and I experienced a problem in our personal relationship shortly after we moved to our present house. Moving house is very stressful, and we were both very tired. My wife Jean and I found ourselves constantly arguing with one another over little things. This can happen in marriage, but we realized eventually that this was not normal, as we were arguing constantly. It was the Lord who alerted us both to the need to pray. We began to be aware that there was a spirit causing strife in the house that seemed to be present mostly in our bedroom, which is where many of the arguments happened.

The Lord prompted us to think why the previous owner had sold the house to us. The woman who sold us the house was divorced, but she and her ex-husband had bought the house together. This indicated that the marriage had broken down whilst they had lived in this house together. We did not know for certain, but we suspected that adultery had taken place, and there was also other evidence of a lifestyle that was ungodly.

We then knew what to do. We thanked the Lord for the woman who had sold us this nice house and we forgave her and her ex-husband for the sins that they had both committed that had led to the breakdown of their marriage and had opened the house to visitation by evil spirits. We then took authority over the spirit causing strife and over other things that the Lord revealed to us and commanded every demonic spirit to leave the bedroom and every part of the house. The difference was amazing! The atmosphere suddenly lifted and Jean and I were restored to our normal relationship.

The spirit of Freemasonry

The third example concerns a friend of mine who is the vicar of a parish church in Lancashire. At the time of this incident I was associate pastor of a nearby church and we were both learning to discern and to deal with the powers of darkness. We attended the very first deliverance ministry training course that Peter Horrobin taught at Ellel Grange in 1987. So much of what Peter said as he taught about demonic powers rang bells with both of us. We were already beginning to reflect on our pastoral experience in the light of this teaching.

My friend felt he was preaching to a brick wall, and discerned that he had to deal with the stronghold of Freemasonry. The founding fathers of his church were practicing Freemasons, and Freemasonry funerals had been regularly conducted there.

I met my friend at the church, accompanied by one of the churchwardens and a lay reader. The vicar and others knelt down at the Communion rail, while I stood behind it. The vicar was to lead the prayers, as he was in authority there. I suggested the issues that needed prayer. We thanked God for all the good things that had come from the founding fathers and all members of the church, including previous vicars. We forgave the fathers and any others for their practice of Freemasonry and the effects of this upon the life of the church. The vicar then commanded the spirit of Freemasonry to leave his church.

At this very moment something unusual happened. The churchwarden tried to speak out the word "help" but he could hardly speak in his normal voice. The Lord immediately gave revelation to me, and I commanded the spirit of Freemasonry to get off this man. He breathed deeply and his voice returned to normal. He told us that when the vicar had ordered the spirit of Freemasonry to go, he had felt a weight upon his head that pressed in upon him so that he felt himself being pushed down and about to lose consciousness. Incidentally, he was kneeling in the very spot where the vicar had sensed such darkness, the door next to his vestry, through which he walked every time he was to conduct a church service.

The spirit of Culloden

I met Bob on one of our many church visits. He had asked for prayer following the Sunday morning service. Bob had been an alcoholic and had many problems in his life, but he had found faith in Christ and was working through these. Whilst on holiday, he had recently visited a very famous battle site in the highlands of Scotland called Culloden Moor, which has become something of a monument to the Scottish dead.

Culloden Moor, which lies in the highlands of Scotland, witnessed the defeat of Bonnie Prince Charlie, otherwise known as the "Young Pretender". In 1746 he and his forces were defeated there by the Duke of Cumberland, and the Jacobite movement came to an end. Bob told me, with a concerned look, that he had felt drawn to this battle site for many years without knowing why. He told me, "It was like a magnet drawing me. It was difficult to put my feelings into words. It was as if I had been there before. I felt sadness and anger, the anger being the strongest feeling. I kept asking why, why, why?"

I knew enough to realize that he needed deliverance from the demonic powers that had gained entry into his family following this bloodthirsty battle. Bob did not know at the time that I prayed for him that his ancestors were present at the battle. One of his Christian names was Mackinnon. He subsequently discovered that this was the family that had raised the standard at the battle of Culloden. This was the name of the spirit that manifested in Bob when I prayed for his deliverance. It actually spoke out of him, challenging my authority. Bob had never been to Culloden Moor before but this demonic familial spirit of Mackinnon had clearly been in one of his ancestors who actually fought at this battle, as Bob was later able to confirm. The Lord was gracious to us and after some persistence the spirit was cast out of Bob. This has made a profound difference in his life, which you can see by reading his personal testimony.

Bob's testimony

I was brought up in a small remote mining village in Scotland. On reflection the village was a strange place: insular and very close knit. As I look back to my childhood and the environment in which I lived, I can now see that there was a demonic principality over the village and the people who lived there, including me and my family.

The door to this demonic invasion was opened, I believe, through poverty and the working and living conditions and the control the coal barons had over the people which was total and obscene. There is a huge spirit of death, which still hangs over the village, and reflects in the lives and attitudes of the villagers. The curse of rejection is everywhere. Sometimes, when I return to the village, I can see the look of hopelessness and grief in people whose faces I now do not recognize. Men and women in their forties and fifties act and look like men and women in their late sixties. Sadly, I believe that in many towns and villages all over Scotland the same scenario exists.

My nation, all through its history, suffered terrible poverty and death. I thank God that He has set me free from this bondage. I was delivered "literally", in great part, by the author of this book to whom I will be forever grateful.

I grew up, not knowing that I was being influenced, almost to the point of destruction, by these things that I have described above. I, like most Scots people, had a great love and passion for my country, its beauty, history etc. On reflection this was never godly or even healthy and caused me great pain at times. I used to long to see the highlands of Scotland where all my heroes, Bruce, Wallace, and Charlie etc. had lived and fought.

My hatred of the English was paramount, to the point that when I heard the word "England" I could feel anger rise within me. I believe God must have a sense of humor because he used an Englishman to deliver and set me free from these demonic influences. Praise God that I can honestly now say as a Christian: God bless all English people, in fact, many of my dearest friends today are English. That, for me, is freedom. How did it happen?

I had suspicions for a long time about my over-zealous national pride. Even when I became a Christian it did not subside and I knew that my feelings towards the English were wrong and certainly not Christian. I knew that I needed deliverance from the demonic influences which I had inherited from my ancestors.

The evidence of this was never more tangible than when my wife and I first visited Culloden Moor, scene of the terrible battle of 1746. As we wandered around the battlefield I had a strange feeling that I had been here before. I felt very uncomfortable, angry, sad and frightened. It was as if I had no control over my feelings. The following morning, in the B & B, an American was having a discussion with another couple about the battle when I suddenly had an uncontrollable urge to tell them what it meant to have been involved in that battle, the pain and suffering etc., but above all to let them know it needn't have happened. I turned to them and in an angry voice vented my feelings on these poor people who immediately went quiet and pretended to eat their porridge! My wife was understandably embarrassed and said afterwards that I was "like a demented man". She was nearer the truth than she realized. Why did I react in this way? Let me explain.

My middle name is Mackinnon. Sometime later, whilst on the island of Iona, I decided to try and find out about my ancestors, who came from Iona. I managed to contact an old gentleman, 98 years of age, who still had all his faculties. He told me that he remembered the Mackinnons and showed me where my grandmother's cottage was. I thanked him for his help and nearly fell over when he told me the Mackinnons had helped raise the standard at the battle of Culloden. This was the first time I had ever heard this and it had a great impact on me. I now knew why I had felt and acted as I did at Culloden Moor. The demonic sources had come down from my Scottish ancestors. My wife's words came back to me: "like a man demented".

Whilst receiving ministry for this, Ken Hepworth came against the spirit of the Clan Mackinnon and as he sat in front of me I had an overwhelming urge to smash his spectacles into his eyes. It was frightening. I could hardly control myself. Another man, in the ministry situation, saw what was about to happen and I was restrained. In due course I was delivered from the evil influences which had come down my family lines. It was a very difficult and painful ministry for me but it was worth every minute to be free of all that evil from the past.

There were some Scottish regiments who were actually fighting on the side of the Duke of Cumberland, for it was in reality a battle for the throne of Great Britain between Protestants and Roman Catholics from the houses of Hanover and Stuart. To this day there is a need for forgiveness and reconciliation between the various Scottish clans and also the Highlanders and the Lowlanders.

Cumberland's dragoons have given the Scottish another reason to hate the English. Following the victory, they went through the town slaughtering men, women and children who had nothing to do with the battle. The British government then banned the Highland way of life. For example the wearing of the kilt and the playing of bagpipes was forbidden. Highlanders were executed or sent to the colonies. You can understand how this affects Scottish feelings even to this day. Hostile feelings resulting from ancient battles live long in the memory of successive generations, which is what seemingly fuels the continuing strife in Northern Ireland today. Clearly Satan and his demonic hoards are behind this destruction of human life and the hatred that follows, but demons cannot act in this way apart from the involvement of human beings, for they need to feed on strong negative emotions such as fear and anger. Hatred is at the root of much satanic activity; the exact opposite of God's nature.

Church leaders experience spiritual breakthrough

I once attended a pastor's prayer meeting at a town hall in a typical local community in Ontario, Canada. This was not their usual venue. The mayor, who had recently come to faith in Christ, invited the spiritual leaders of his township to pray for him and the elected officials that they might know God's blessing and direction, particularly in the moral realm. Following this time of prayer, one of the pastors led a communion service in the basement of the town hall. This was an amazing event. The spiritual and civic powers joined together for the purpose of seeking God's blessing. The pastors themselves were enjoying good fellowship together and were in unity. To get to this place of unity and blessing is not easy, so how did it come about? I believe that the events I am about to relate to you reveal the reasons.

A year previous to this, one of the local church pastors came to see me. He was interested in our teaching on "claiming the ground". There were two things that he wanted: to invite me to share this teaching with the Christian leaders in the town, and to share something that the Lord had laid on his own heart. He told me that the pastors' meeting had discussed the idea of seeking forgiveness from the Roman Catholics in the town for the sins of their Protestant ancestors who had severely persecuted the Catholics and who had hindered the establishment of the very first Roman Catholic church in that town. In particular they wanted to confess their sin in setting fire to the building. They didn't wish to apologize for the Reformation or for Protestant doctrine, but only to confess the sins of their ancestors. Some months after this visit to my office and after much prayer, a special service took place in the Roman Catholic church where one of the pastors, representing the Protestant churches in the town, confessed the sins of the ancestors. He then asked the priest and the congregation for their forgiveness, which was freely given. I believe that this was instrumental in changing the spiritual atmosphere over the churches and also made possible the mayor's remarkable request for prayer.

One can expect from the teaching of Scripture that the enemy will do everything he possibly can to attack this kind of unity wherever it exists (Psalm 133; 1 Peter 5:8; Matthew 12:25–26). Sadly, four years after this joining together in prayer, the mayor lost the next election. The pastors who were in such unity are now separated; one of the senior pastors has retired, and some of the others have moved to new churches in different towns. My last conversation with a pastor in this town told me that relationships are not as good as they were and the bad atmosphere over the town has returned.

The creation of a spiritual atmosphere

What is it that creates a spiritual atmosphere? Have you ever sensed the presence of God? As Christians we should expect to experience His living presence when we are meeting together for worship. As our desire for His presence increases, the awareness of the presence of God becomes increasingly strong, and this in turn affects the purity of our worship.

Alternatively, it is possible to experience an evil presence. When I was the director of a former Ellel Ministries center in Canada, a vital part of the work was breaking curses on the land and cleansing the building from evil spirits. The presence of evil spirits was affecting our young people's team, particularly the women. The young women were experiencing nightmares and not getting their proper sleep. Many of them could see eyes in the dark that were peering at them and they were frightened and disturbed. It took us many months to identify the source and eventually to drive away the powers of darkness that were behind this evil activity. It proved to be rooted in the occult practices of the First Nation Peoples (The Red Indians) who had lived on the land at the time when it was being taken from them by the white settlers. They had performed specific rituals that would bring down curses upon those who subsequently lived on the land. After we had confessed the sins of our ancestors against the First Nation Peoples, we ordered the evil spirits to leave the land. Unless we know how to discern the presence of such curses, and how to remove them, we shall inevitably be affected by the bad spiritual atmosphere created through the presence of these evil spirits in the places where we live, work, and worship.

Every place has a "feel" to it or an atmosphere, which can be either good or bad. The character of a property is much more than the physical dimensions of the number and size of the rooms. These and the décor will of course give a certain feel to the property, but the character of the property lies in the spiritual atmosphere which results from the nature of the lives of those who have visited, lived or even fought there. One needs to ask the question: has this land, this building, this work, been opened up to the light of God and His Spirit or perhaps to the darkness of sin and therefore to an evil spirit?

Let us consider a healing center like Ellel Grange as an example. Many people sense the living presence and peace of God, particularly when they visit for the first time. This is because the building has been set apart for the work of the kingdom of God and the team are constantly praying and laboring to fulfil the vision that God gave for the ministry. However, this was not always the case. In the early days of the work one could discern darkness in many different parts of the property. These areas of darkness were systematically cleansed by prayer.

The ground that we occupy either for personal living or for the worship of the one true and living God may be contaminated. It is a commendable practice of some churches to consecrate every new church building prior to its use by Christians. However, just as deliverance from evil spirits for the individual is often a process, so it is also with the deliverance and cleansing of a place of worship. Unless we deal with the rights given to evil spirits through sin, the prayers of consecration will not in themselves rid the place of the presence of unclean spirits. In the measure that the enemy has gained the right to be present, the reign and the presence of Jesus Christ is not as evident as it should be. Furthermore, various sinful activities, for example sexual sin and abuse (which can happen even on church premises) will cause consecrated ground to be re-contaminated. This means that cleansing is not a once and for all activity, unless of course we can ensure absolute holiness amongst the people of God.

Chapter 3

The Curse on the Ground

As curses frequently prevent us from experiencing the fullness of God's blessing, it is essential that we understand the nature of curses as well as the various types. In the process of cleansing churches and the land they are built on, from time to time we shall find ourselves needing to break curses.

The concept of life or death, blessing or curse, is not only a vital principle for the nation of Israel, but also for God's people in all ages (Deuteronomy 30:19–20). The Promised Land given to the Jewish people is unique to them, and is theirs for all time (Exodus 32:13; Deuteronomy 4:1). However, the principle of blessings or curses visiting the land is as relevant for us as it is for them. In the Bible we find on the one hand curses that await God's timing for removal, such as the general curse on the ground (Genesis 3:17), and on the other hand curses that God will remove if we seek Him for the cause and respond appropriately. I shall give examples of both.

Various types of curse

An example of the first kind of curse is to be found in Genesis 3 and concerns the general curse on the ground. This is the curse that followed the first sin of mankind:

> *"Cursed is the ground because of you;*
> *through painful toil you will eat of it*
> *all the days of your life.*
> *It will produce thorns and thistles for you,*
> *and you will eat the plants of the field.*

> *By the sweat of your brow*
> *you will eat your food ... "*   (Genesis 3:17–19a)

What does it mean to say that the earth is cursed? A curse is usually spoken in words and is specific. It can be pronounced by God or man but its application is through Satan and demons. A curse can be described as an invisible spiritual barrier or power that either brings direct and punitive evil results, or at least robs the individual of the fullness of God's blessing. Although a curse is invisible in its application, it is visible in its outworking. For example, the curse on the ground can be seen by looking at thorns and thistles and seeing wheat and tares that grow together in the soil. These weeds which make it difficult for the farmer to reap a rich and full harvest were not present before sin entered the world. The original creation was *"very good"* (Genesis 1:31) and cultivation of the soil was without hard toil. This is no longer the case as the curse on the ground works as a hindrance against man.

Where do curses come from?

The curse on the ground came as a direct result of sin; all curses can be traced to sin. Some curses come as a consequence of breaking God's law (Deuteronomy 27, 28) while other curses are pronounced through evil human intention, as in the attempt of Balak to curse Israel (Numbers 22:5–6). Curses can also come as a result of pronouncements made by authority figures even without evil intention. For example, a father who tells his child, "You are a failure; you will never achieve anything." Scripture says that life and death are in the power of the tongue, and that the tongue can be used either to bless or to curse (Proverbs 18:21; James 3:9).

A person can even curse themselves. Jacob knew that by deceiving his father Isaac he would bring down a curse upon himself (Genesis 27:11–12). His mother Rebekah volunteered to let the curse fall upon herself (Genesis 27:13). Not long after this Rebekah lost her son Jacob as he had to leave the family home in fear of his life from his brother Esau (Genesis 27:42–45). She also became fearful that Jacob would marry a Canaanite woman, which Esau eventually did (Genesis 27:46; 28:6–9).

Before sin entered the world there was only blessing. A curse can indirectly affect the life of man through an inanimate object such as the ground, or it can directly affect man in his own being. This curse on the ground is an example of an indirect curse. One particular characteristic of this curse is that God will not remove it in answer to prayer, and in this respect it is similar to death. Although the power of these troublesome aspects of human life has been thoroughly dealt with through the death and resurrection of Christ, we shall nevertheless have to wait for a future time to see their complete removal. This will happen when Satan is deposed from his place of authority as "god of this world". The general curse upon the earth's fruitfulness can only be removed by God, which He will do when the whole creation, including redeemed mankind, becomes completely free. The Scriptures say that:

> *"The creation waits in eager expectation for the sons of God to be revealed. For the creation was subjected to frustration, not by its own choice, but by the will of the one who subjected it, in hope that the creation itself will be liberated from its bondage to decay and brought into the glorious freedom of the children of God."* (Romans 8:19–21)

However land may have been cursed in addition to this by man. For example, by the First Nation People of North America who have sometimes cursed the land that the white man took from them. We can expect the Lord to remove such curses when the necessary repentance and forgiveness has taken place.

The Jericho curse

Another example of a curse authorized by God which man cannot remove is to be found in the book of Joshua. It is the curse that Joshua pronounced against the rebuilding of the ancient city of Jericho in Joshua 6:26. The curse was attached to an oath, which Joshua pronounced in his capacity as leader of the nation of Israel. The curse applied not only to the existing generation, but also to successive ones. If activated, the curse would result in the death of the eldest and the youngest son of the man who disregarded the oath. It lay dormant for some five hundred and fifty years until the time of King Ahab, for it would take effect only if someone were to go against this solemn oath. Sadly a man called Hiel did so, and this is the result recorded in Scripture:

> *"In Ahab's time, Hiel of Bethel rebuilt Jericho. He laid its foundations at the cost of his firstborn son Abiram, and he set up its gates at the cost of his youngest son Segub, in accordance with the word of the LORD spoken by Joshua son of Nun."*
>
> (1 Kings 16:34)

The curse on the Gibeonites

The following example brings the two types of curse together. It concerns the Gibeonites who were all cursed with life-long servitude for the whole of their lives following their deception of Joshua and the elders of Israel (Joshua 9:23). The effect of this curse meant that they would never be able to be anything other than woodcutters and water carriers as long as they remained a people. However, there were some real benefits for the Gibeonites. Firstly their lives were spared, and secondly the Israelites and the Gibeonites were now bound together as one people by the treaty of peace that they had entered into (Joshua 9:15). Israel's enemies were the Gibeonites' enemies, and vice versa. Therefore, when Gibeon was attacked by five great nations, Israel was obliged by the treaty to march out to war in order to protect them, which they did by completely defeating King Adoni-Zedek and the other kings (Joshua 10:1–15).

Israel's famine in King David's time

Some years later Israel experienced a famine that lasted for three years, and David inquired of the Lord (2 Samuel 21:1–14). The Lord told him that the famine was caused by the murder of the Gibeonites by King Saul, an event that must have happened early in Saul's reign as Israel's first king. Even though Saul who committed the sin was now dead, it remained that innocent blood had been shed and needed to be atoned for (Genesis 9:6). The surviving Gibeonites asked for the death of seven of Saul's sons (2 Samuel 21:5–6). This request was clearly in accord with the Bible's teaching about the only means of cleansing the ground following the shedding of innocent blood (Genesis 9:6; Numbers 35:33). It was not until these seven were put to death that God answered David's prayer on behalf of the land (2 Samuel 21:14) and the blessing of God returned. The Lord removed the curse, and He cleansed and healed the land.

From these Scriptures we learn a number of important characteristics of a curse:

- A curse is formulated through the spoken word
- A curse continues to do its work until it is cancelled out
- A curse can remain active even though dormant for many generations
- A curse has power to affect successive generations
- Some curses can be removed through prayer and some cannot
- Only the Lord has the power to remove a curse

The original curse on the ground (Genesis 3:17) has been reinforced through much sin over many generations. We need now to consider what the Scriptures teach on how curses gain access if we are to be effective in removing them from the ground on which we live and worship.

Defilement of the land through innocent bloodshed

"Do not pollute the land where you are. Bloodshed pollutes the land, and atonement cannot be made for the land on which blood has been shed, except by the blood of the one who shed it. Do not defile the land where you live and where I dwell, for I, the LORD, dwell among the Israelites."

(Numbers 35:33–34)

The very first case of the shedding of innocent blood was the death of Abel recorded in the book of Genesis (Genesis 4:10). Cain feared that someone would seek to avenge the death of his brother by killing him (Genesis 4:13–15), but at this time in history the Lord did not enforce the death penalty. However, this sin of murder brought Cain under the power of a specific curse (Genesis 4:11). From that day forth when he cultivated the ground it would no longer yield its strength to him (Genesis 4:12 NASB). Bearing in mind that the ground was already cursed because of human sin, what we are seeing is an increase of the curse upon the ground, but affecting only Cain and his descendants. Generations later, as the human population multiplied on the earth, there was an increase of corruption and the earth became full of violence. At this time God decided to punish the world for its sin and He sent a worldwide flood (Genesis 6:11). It was not until Noah came out of the Ark that the death penalty was instituted (Genesis 9:6). The death of the murderer was required to remove the defilement of the land.

So important was this removal of defilement that provision was made to atone for the death of a victim when the identity of the murderer could not be established (Deuteronomy 21:1–9). Let us ask the question: how many murders have not been atoned for since those days, especially in the late twentieth century? How defiled is the earth as a consequence? According to the Old Testament, atonement for the land can only be made by the shedding of the blood of the murderer (Genesis 9:6; Numbers 35:33). Whether or not we have been right in our generation to remove the death penalty will perhaps only be known when we face God. However, I am certain that where murder has not been atoned for in the prescribed way, atonement and cleansing for the land can be obtained on the basis of the death of Christ.

The murder of a schoolboy

In the late seventies when I worked with SASRA (The Soldiers and Airmen's Scripture Readers Association), I was stationed in Germany where I lived with my wife and children. During this time there was a horrible murder near an army barracks, which I used to visit in my capacity as an Army Scripture Reader. The Anglican chaplain was asked by the parents of the murdered boy to pray at the spot where their son lost his life. He asked me to accompany him, although I had never done anything like this before. We went to the derelict house where the boy had been murdered. The place where the boy had been killed was stained by blood.

The chaplain and I were deeply moved as we thought about

the way in which this boy was killed and considered the last moments of his life. We prayed for the person or people who had committed this act of murder. What remains with me is the memory of the sense of evil that was present. At that time I did not understand that an event like this opens a place up to the presence of evil spirits. From experience in ministry gained over the years of ministering into the high levels of the occult world, I see now that it is possible or even likely that demonic powers were behind this murder.

More than a coincidence

A few years ago in Canada I was asked to go and pray for a couple who were desperately in need of prayer. Their house had burnt down and they were fearful of moving into a newly rebuilt house on the site. The husband was very depressed and the wife had lost her joy and zest for life. The amazing thing was that this was the second time their house had burnt down on exactly the same spot! The first time it happened they were both asleep in bed. The wife, who has no sense of smell, awoke to the sound of crackling fire on the roof, and they just managed to escape from the house. The second time it was on a Sunday and they were at church! I had gathered a small team together and we began to ask the couple some questions about themselves and the history of the land, after which we began to pray to the Lord for His revelation.

We tried to discover if there were any curses operating in the lives of this dear couple, but couldn't find anything that would point to destruction by fire. We discovered that the houses that had burnt down had also been occupied by another family living in the basement. Had they done anything to open the house to destruction? It was thought that this was a possibility as they were not Christians, but nothing specific was known.

One of the team had a revelation of fire in the grounds, which prompted another team member to recount the history of the ground. The house was built on reclaimed land that had previously been swamp land, on which there was a constant burning of the swamp grass. This still didn't seem to be the answer. We continued to pray and further revelation came that there had been a human sacrifice on the property.

We asked the Lord to confirm this and as we prayed and walked over the ground a deep conviction grew within each of us that this was indeed the revelation that we needed from the Lord.

As we stood on the land next to the house, the couple invited Jesus to be Lord of their own lives and of the land and home. The husband forgave the couple with whom they had shared their home for anything that they had done which had given demons access. He then forgave those who had committed the sin of human sacrifice and for the fire that had destroyed their two houses. We asked the Lord to deal with the human aspect of the sacrifice and the husband then took authority over the evil spirits that had gained access to his land to cause the fire, and ordered them to leave his property. We supported him in prayer for some time. We finished our prayer time by going into the house and inviting the presence of the Lord into every part of the house. We left and shortly afterwards the couple moved into the completed house. This was over five years ago and today this couple are still rejoicing in the Lord with a joy and zest for life!

Defilement of the land from human sacrifice
A Canaanite practice that was both abhorrent and forbidden by God was child sacrifice:

> *"Do not give any of your children to be sacrificed to Molech, for you must not profane the name of your God. I am the LORD."*
> (Leviticus 18:21)

The Lord made it very clear to Israel, that whoever committed this evil practice was to be put to death, and that to protect such a person was to invite the death penalty (Leviticus 20:1–5). Molech was the god of the Ammonites who was worshiped through the sacrifice of children. This was common practice in Phoenicia and the surrounding nations. Sadly Israel did not obey God in this matter. Even King Solomon built a high place on a hill east of Jerusalem for the worship of *"the detestable god of the Ammonites"* (1 Kings 11:4–8). King Manasseh actually sacrificed his sons to Molech (2 Chronicles 33:6). The sacrifice of children was one of the reasons that

God sent the Israelites into captivity (Jeremiah 32:35–36). The practice of human sacrifice brings great defilement to the land. Such an evil practice gives an open door to Satan and demonic powers.

The spirit of abortion

Today the practice of abortion is widespread and available in many countries. Some nations use abortion as a means of controlling the birth rate. In the United Kingdom, abortion has increased enormously since a British member of parliament, David (now Lord) Steel, introduced the Abortion Act in 1967. Since this became law, more than five million unborn babies have been put to death. We were told that the bill would protect women from back street abortionists and that its introduction wouldn't increase the number of abortions. Sadly, this has not been the case. How will God judge a society that kills its most vulnerable members? How much has this sin polluted the land? What rights have demonic powers been given over our towns and our cities through this wickedness? There seems little difference in terminating the life of an unborn child through the National Health Service on the altars of lust and inconvenience than on the altar of Molech! The day is coming when the earth will conceal its murdered victims no longer and then the Lord will punish the unrepentant people of the earth for these hidden sins (Isaiah 26:20–21). It is clear from personal experience in ministry to many women who have had an abortion that they need a lot of inner healing and deliverance from demons, in particular the spirit of death. Thank God that Jesus has compassion on those who have participated in this sin and that through the cross there is forgiveness, healing and deliverance for those who have been deceived into having an abortion. If a woman's womb can be visited by the spirit of death following an abortion, so can the building where the abortion has taken place.

The concept of defilement

Why should blood, an organic substance, defile or pollute the land? There is something here that needs further examination. It is always significant when human beings lose their lives. Murder is contrary to God's law and a gross violation of the individual. Each human being is made in the image and after the likeness of God (Genesis 1:26–27). Because Satan is a murderer (John 8:44), he encourages the act of murder, which gives him powerful rights to visit the place where the murder occurred with unclean spirits, in order to defile that place and attack human beings. The presence of unclean spirits causes continuing defilement.

The water of cleansing

It is worth noting that provision for cleansing following contact with a dead body was given in the law:

> "Whoever touches the dead body of anyone will be unclean for seven days. He must purify himself with the water on the third day and on the seventh day; then he will be clean. But if he does not purify himself on the third and seventh days, he will not be clean. Whoever touches the dead body of anyone and fails to purify himself defiles the LORD's tabernacle. That person must be cut off from Israel. Because the water of cleansing has not been sprinkled on him, he is unclean; his uncleanness remains on him.
>
> This is the law that applies when a person dies in a tent: Anyone who enters the tent and anyone who is in it will be unclean for seven days, and every open container without a lid fastened on it will be unclean.
>
> Anyone out in the open who touches someone who has been killed with a sword or someone who has died a natural death, or anyone who touches a human bone or a grave, will be unclean for seven days."   (Numbers 19:11–16)

Why would physical contact with the dead cause defilement? At first you might think that the issue is one of the spread of disease which was transferred through contact with the dead body. While it may include this, the scope is much wider. A man who dies on a battlefield from a fatal wound is unlikely to transmit disease and neither is someone who has died from natural causes! So what causes defilement? Ask yourself the question, "Where do demons go when the person whom they inhabit dies?" The answer is that they look for another home, preferably human. It is unclean spirits that make a person unclean. Cleansing in the Old Testament was through following the prescribed ritual of purification as in Numbers 19. When they followed this procedure they were cleansed and delivered from any demons that had transferred to them.

Defilement of the land through sexual sin

When preparing the Israelites to go into the Promised Land, the Lord warned them not to commit the same sexual sins as the Canaanites. Following a list of sexual sins, this is what the Lord then said through Moses:

> *"Do not defile yourselves in any of these ways, because this is how the nations that I am going to drive out before you became defiled. Even the land was defiled, so I punished it for its sin, and the land vomited out its inhabitants. But you must keep my decrees and my laws. The native-born and the aliens living among you must not do any of these detestable things. For all these things were done by the people who lived in the land before you, and the land became defiled."*
>
> (Leviticus 18:24–28)

Here we see that the land the Israelites were to live in had been defiled by the Canaanites through sexual sin. The Israelites were warned not to commit the same sins, otherwise God would judge them as He had done the Canaanites, and the land would vomit them out as well. We are not told exactly how the land can become defiled through sexual sin. It is likely that this would have been evident to the people living at that time, who would have some understanding that sin could give access to unclean spirits and as a consequence defile the ground (Leviticus 17:7; Deuteronomy 32:16–17; Psalm 106:37).

God's holiness is offended by the act of sin and His wrath is stirred, but in addition, it is also an affront to God that unclean spirits are given liberty to roam the land. This is particularly offensive to God in respect of land that He especially claims as His own. When in Scripture the Lord refers to the Promised Land that He gave to the Israelites, He describes it as "My Land" (2 Chronicles 7:20; Joel 3:2). The

Lord dwells among His people and consequently they are warned to avoid all uncleanness (Leviticus 5:3; Numbers 35:34). What significance does this have today for us, also a people in covenant relationship with God?

Defilement of the land through idolatry
The practice of idolatry is in reality the worship of demons. It invites the presence of demons; hence both the place and the people who worship will become demonized. In the New Testament Paul warns against participating in idol feasts (1 Corinthians 10:14–22). Whilst he teaches that an idol in itself is nothing, he also teaches that to sacrifice to an idol is actually to make an offering to a demon. Paul taught that it is not right to participate with demons through sharing in both the Lord's Supper and in idolatrous feasts. In the Psalms there is a revealing reference to the practice of child sacrifice:

> *"They did not destroy the peoples*
> *as the LORD had commanded them,*
> *but they mingled with the nations*
> *and adopted their customs.*
> *They worshiped their idols,*
> *which became a snare to them.*
> *They sacrificed their sons*
> *and their daughters to demons.*
> *They shed innocent blood,*
> *the blood of their sons and daughters,*
> *whom they sacrificed to the idols of Canaan,*
> *and the land was desecrated by their blood.*
> *They defiled themselves by what they did;*
> *by their deeds they prostituted themselves.*
> *Therefore the LORD was angry with his people*
> *and abhorred his inheritance.*
> *He handed them over to the nations,*
> *and their foes ruled over them.*
> *Their enemies oppressed them*
> *and subjected them to their power.*
> *Many times he delivered them,*
> *but they were bent on rebellion*
> *and they wasted away in their sin."*   (Psalm 106:34–43)

Unclean creatures

Isaiah prophesied that Babylon would be overthrown and that no one would live there, leaving it the haunt of unclean creatures such as jackals, owls, wild goats, and hyenas. The term "wild goats" is linked with the worship of demons (Leviticus 17:7; 2 Chronicles 11:15). It is possible that the mention of unclean animals in the Old Testament is similar to their mention in the New Testament. When Jesus gave His disciples authority to trample on snakes and scorpions He wasn't referring to wild animals! His comment was in relation to the joy that the disciples experienced in casting out demons (Luke 10:18). Possibly all unclean animals are associated with demons. In the book of Revelation, Babylon is described as, *"a home for demons, and a haunt for every evil spirit . . . "* (Revelation 18:2).

The history of the church in England

As disciples of Jesus we live and worship on land which has been defiled. Every piece of land has a history that began long before anything was built upon it. For example ancient Britain was home to the Celtic religion of Druidism. Stonehenge on Salisbury Plain is the ruin of a former Druid Temple. History records that Pope Gregory the First sent Augustine, a Benedictine Abbot, along with thirty other monks, as missionaries to England. In the year AD 596 Philip Schaff, in his *History of the Christian Church* made the following comments:

> "He directs the missionaries not to destroy the heathen temples, but to convert them into Christian churches, to substitute the worship of relics for the worship of idols, and to allow the new converts, on the day of dedication and other festivities, to kill cattle according to their ancient custom, yet no more to the devils, but to the praise of God; for it is impossible, he thought, to efface everything at once from their obdurate minds; and he who endeavors to ascend to the highest place, must rise by degrees or steps, and not by leaps. This method was faithfully followed by his missionaries. It no doubt facilitated the nominal conversion of England, but swept

a vast amount of heathenism into the Christian church, which it took centuries to eradicate."

(Philip Schaff, *History of the Christian Church*)

Some of our ancient parish churches have been built on former Druidic temple sites. Since ancient Druids practiced human sacrifice, it is not difficult to see the need for cleansing and deliverance of the ground upon which these evil acts took place.

Judgement by fire

Since sin entered the world through the human race, mankind has sown much wickedness through many generations, and the earth has become an unclean place. The Israelites were told that certain sins would pollute or defile the land in which they lived. Sadly they committed all those sins. The prophet Isaiah said:

> *"The earth is also polluted by its inhabitants, for they transgressed laws, violated statutes, broke the everlasting covenant."* (Isaiah 24:5, NASB)

In the last days the earth will have become so unclean that nothing short of the coming judgement of God's fire will cleanse it:

> *"By the same word the present heavens and earth are reserved for fire, being kept for the day of judgement and destruction of ungodly men ... But the day of the Lord will come like a thief. The heavens will disappear with a roar; the elements will be destroyed by fire, and the earth and everything in it will be laid bare."* (2 Peter 3:7, 10)

In the meantime it is imperative that we reclaim the ground from the enemy where he has had access through sin. Before we consider that however, we need to understand the concept of holy ground.

Chapter 4

The Concept of Holy Ground

Having established a biblical foundation for understanding curses and how they work, we now need to consider the concept of holy ground. This concept is clearly stated in the Old Testament. For some Christians this is not a new idea, as they are in denominations that include the practice of consecrating their places of worship. However, what we also need to recognize is that if demonic powers do not necessarily leave a believer at conversion, then they may not leave a building when it is consecrated, especially if they are not ordered to leave by those in authority. Therefore, we need to learn how to cleanse and deliver a consecrated building from evil spirits as well as how to set it apart as holy for worship. The Lord has provided powerful spiritual weapons for us to use in the pulling down of demonic strongholds. With these weapons we can overcome all the power of the enemy that he might use against the church, its leaders, its people, and its mission (2 Corinthians 10:3–5; Luke 10:17–19).

The holiness of God's presence

God's requirement for His people and the places where He lives amongst us is holiness (Leviticus 11:44; 20:7; Hebrews 12:14; 2 Peter 3:11). Although the Lord is omnipresent, His presence is also manifested in specific places and at certain times (Exodus 19:9). Whenever the Lord is present that place becomes holy. However, the Lord will only manifest the glory of His presence where His holiness is welcomed and His people are prepared.

> *"And the* LORD *said to Moses, 'Go to the people and consecrate them today and tomorrow. Have them wash their clothes and be ready by the third day, because on that day the* LORD *will come down on Mount Sinai in the sight of all the people.'"*
>
> (Exodus 19:10–11)

> *"Even the priests, who approach the* LORD, *must consecrate themselves, or the* LORD *will break out against them."*
>
> (Exodus 19:22)

Mount Sinai the holy mountain

We need to turn to the book of Exodus to understand the concept of holy ground. In Exodus 19 Moses and the Israelites were camped at the foot of Mount Sinai, one of the mountains in the range called Horeb. Moses is summoned by the Lord to go up the mountain to meet with Him. God spoke to him and told him that He would come down the mountain so that the people would hear Him (Exodus 19:9; Hebrews 12:18–21). In preparation for this the people needed to consecrate themselves and the mountain had to be cordoned off (Exodus 19:12). This was to prevent both man and animal from touching it, as the presence of the Lord made the mountain holy. The Lord told Moses that if anyone did touch the mountain, the penalty was death.

> *"Moses said to the* LORD, *'The people cannot come up Mount Sinai, because you yourself warned us, "Put limits around the mountain and set it apart as holy".'"* (Exodus 19:23)

The mountain became holy through the Lord's presence; anything that God sets apart becomes holy. God descended upon the mountain to meet with Moses for a limited time and a specific purpose. He shared His laws and the details of how to build the tabernacle with Moses.

The burning bush

The book of Exodus records another example of how common, unclean ground becomes holy ground when the Lord manifests His presence:

> *"There the angel of the* Lord *appeared to him in flames of fire from within a bush. Moses saw that though the bush was on fire it did not burn up. So Moses thought, 'I will go over and see this strange sight – why the bush does not burn up.' When the* Lord *saw that he had gone over to look, God called to him from within the bush, 'Moses! Moses!' And Moses said, 'Here I am.' 'Do not come any closer,' God said. 'Take off your sandals, for the place where you are standing is holy ground.' Then he said, 'I am the God of your father, the God of Abraham, the God of Isaac and the God of Jacob.' At this, Moses hid his face, because he was afraid to look at God."*
>
> (Exodus 3:2–6)

God spoke to Moses from the burning bush and told him to take the sandals off his feet because he was standing on holy ground. The ground was not holy apart from God's presence, as it was common ground, but it had become holy because of a visitation from God Himself. The audible voice of God spoke from the burning bush and told Moses, *"Do not come any closer ... Take off your sandals, for the place where you are standing is holy ground"*. It was common practice among Egyptian priests and throughout the East, when entering a temple, to remove the shoes as a confession of personal defilement and conscious unworthiness. Moses would have been familiar with this idea. It was entirely appropriate that the living God should require this act of reverence if Moses was to stand in His presence. He alone is the Holy One (Joshua 24:19; 1 Samuel 6:20; Mark 1:24). The act of removing one's shoes was also an act of reverence and submission. In this particular instance it was an acknowledgement that the place Moses was standing on was holy ground.

A heavenly visitor

Joshua 5 records another similar visit by the Lord. Prior to the fall of Jericho, Joshua had an unusual visitor. When he was near Jericho, he looked up and saw a man standing before him with a sword in His hand that He was clearly ready to use. Joshua asked Him whose side He was on. The Man's reply indicates that He was not a man and Joshua's response indicates that it was not an angel, but the Lord Himself. He came as Commander of the army of the Lord. At this Joshua fell face down on the ground in reverence. Joshua was told, *"Take off your sandals, for the place where you are standing is holy"* (Joshua 5:15). The reason that the ground became holy was because God the Son had come from heaven and placed His feet upon this earth. The area surrounding His presence had therefore become holy.

Consumed by holy fire

God's presence can also be manifested in the holy fire of His judgement, not only against unbelievers as in the case of Sodom and Gomorrah, but also against disobedient believers such as the sons of Nadab and Abihu, who disobeyed the Lord by adding something extra in their censers as a fire offering to Him (Genesis 19; Leviticus 10:1–2). The sons of Korah were also consumed by fire from the Lord's presence because of their rebellion against Him (Numbers 16). The fire of God's judgement also consumed some Israelites who complained about their hardships in the desert (Numbers 11:1–3).

God inhabits the praises of His people (Psalm 22:3, KJV). It is His presence that we seek as we come together in worship. We all know what it is like to try and worship in an atmosphere that is heavy and oppressive. It is my desire that as we apply the scriptural principles within this book, the Lord may fill our churches continually with His holy presence. Let our churches and our hearts be filled with His truth and light.

> *"Yet a time is coming and has now come when the true worshippers will worship the Father in spirit and truth, for they are the kind of worshippers the Father seeks. God is spirit, and his worshippers must worship in spirit and in truth."*
> (John 4:23–24)

Other "holy" places

In the light of this truth, let us ask a question. Should a Christian disciple visit an Islamic mosque, a Sikh, or Hindu temple? It is common practice amongst those training to be RE teachers, missionaries or those preparing for the ordained ministry to visit the local mosque as part of their training. Also, many Christians visit these temples when on holiday. It may have already occurred to you that when going into these temples the visitor has to take off his or her shoes! The action of taking off one's shoes is a declaration that one is entering a holy place, and recognizing the spirit in the temple. That is certainly how the demons will see it.

It is not the same as entering someone's house and taking your shoes off at the door. This is not seen as an act of worship, because you are not entering a temple or place of worship. It is a kindness to the host to keep his carpet or floor clean. When going into a religious temple the same action says something very different. There is recognition of the spirit in the temple, which you are honoring by the removal of your shoes. We have discovered through a lot of experience in ministry that believers who visit these temples for whatever reason are likely to need deliverance from the spirit of Islam or whatever spirit was associated with the particular religion of the temple visited. On a number of occasions I have cast out a spirit of Islam from Christians who have visited Islamic Mosques whilst on holiday. I have also cast out religious spirits from an ex-Bible student who went to a reputable Bible college. As part of her course, which included a unit on comparative religion, she visited mosques and temples, and of course she took off her shoes upon entering these places. The one true and living God, Father, Son and Holy Spirit is neither recognized nor worshiped in the temples of other religions.

These temples are not filled with the light of truth but with the deception and darkness of Satan. One could perhaps visit a mosque or temple and be protected from the demonic spirit, but you would have to keep your shoes on. It is unlikely that admittance would be given to someone not willing to take off his or her shoes. In fact it would be seen as disrespectful to their religion. We can respect all men regardless of color or creed, but we cannot recognize their god as the same as our God. To do so is to be guilty of the sin of idolatry. I shall return to this subject in a later chapter when looking at the consequences of interfaith services that have taken place in Christian cathedrals.

Evil spirits in the church sanctuary

Some years ago I conducted a healing weekend in an Anglican church in England. The vicar told me that he often preached from the front of the sanctuary and not from his pulpit. He did this so that he might be closer to his congregation. Another reason was that he always felt uncomfortable standing anywhere in his sanctuary. Amazingly, he felt unwelcome, as if he shouldn't be there, even though he was in his own church! This had the effect of adding to his high level of rejection from early childhood.

After discussion and prayer together we felt the Lord directing us to the bell tower, and we thought we should go up as far as we could. We both climbed a very narrow winding stairway to the floor underneath the bell tower, which of course was directly over the sanctuary. This place felt unfriendly to say the least. On the floor we saw evidence of dead animals laid out in what seemed to be a pattern. Often people in the occult will kill animals in the course of a specific ritual in order to direct curses against the church leader and his people. We asked the Lord for confirmation, and we prayed specifically into this as we were led by the Holy Spirit.

First the vicar proclaimed that Jesus is the Lord of the Church universal and then he invited Jesus to be Lord of every part of the church building, of himself as the leader, of the work of the church, and also to be Lord over its people. This might seem to be a foregone conclusion. However, when dealing with the powers of darkness it is always necessary to proclaim the truth.

Next he forgave any person or people who had wished him and his people harm by seeking to curse them. He then took authority over every demonic power that was present and ordered it to leave his church. We also prayed in the sanctuary and broke some Freemasonry curses. Some time after the weekend he noticed the bad atmosphere had gone and he felt comfortable being in the church sanctuary.

Using the authority God has given

The Lord has given the keys of the kingdom to His disciples and those in leadership need to use them (Matthew 16:19; 18:18). An aspect of this truth is reflected in the service that takes place when a new vicar in the Anglican Church is installed or instituted. During the service, which is conducted by the bishop, the archdeacon leads the new vicar to the chancel steps to be presented by the churchwarden with the keys of the church and the parsonage house, together with the church inventory. This is a spiritual statement that the new incumbent has been given spiritual authority to act in this local church. What he lets in comes in and has a right to be there, what he forbids has no right to be there. It is not only Anglican pastors who have this kind of authority; I believe God intends every church leader to have this authority by their appointment as pastor.

A new church building

Seven years after its beginning, a new church in the UK had grown to the point where the members were able to buy their own facility, and be removed from their commitment to rental of a school premises for the Sunday services. The building that the Lord led them to was previously the home of the town rugby club. This had been the venue for many bawdy drinking parties and all the behavior normally associated with drunkenness. The atmosphere was less than holy. The following is a testimony from the pastor, who is a personal friend of mine, about how the Lord changed the spiritual atmosphere of their new building and brought blessings after they prayed specifically about their inherited spiritual problem.

Testimony

When we bought the building, it had been previously used as a rugby club. Because the actual pitch was a couple of miles away, the club tried to make ends meet by hiring the building out for functions. These frequently ended in brawls to which the police had to be called. The club began to get into financial difficulties, and so staff began putting their hand into the till, and the club soon went bust. There was also a death on the premises a few years previously. With the club going bust, the building lay empty for about a year. In that time, there were numerous break-ins, vandalism, fires being started and so on. When we bought the building and started to renovate it, local kids assured us that they would just fire-bomb the place, and the glazing company told us that we would be crazy to have new windows put in, because they would most likely be smashed before the job was completed!

As we prayed over the building, we were given a picture of the building with a giant octopus on top of it, with its tentacles reaching down over the building and out into the neighborhood. We prayed into this, and the Lord revealed that the tentacles represented various curses over the building: the curse of death, financial mismanagement, violence, bankruptcy, hatred, fear (and a couple of other minor issues). We took authority over each of these "tentacles" and spoke death to them in the name of the Lord. In place of each we prayed the opposite: life, financial integrity and blessing, love and peace. We went from room to room in the building, praying over and anointing the doorposts of each room and speaking God's presence into every corner of the building.

Since then, around forty people have found faith in Christ. We were also able to buy the building with no debt, and remain debt free! Despite being an independent, fairly small church, many people have found healing and new hope ... and not a single window has been smashed.

The importance of dedicating a building for Christian worship

A building for Christian worship needs to be separated from common usage, and purified from all evil. When a place for Christian worship is properly dedicated and consecrated (set apart to the service of the living God) it becomes a place where He manifests His living presence. The dedication changes the use of the building from a common to a divine purpose, from being unholy to becoming holy. It is an invitation to the Lord and also a declaration to Satan and the powers of darkness, that the ground upon which the building stands is holy ground, and the activities within its walls are holy activities. When accompanied by deliverance from evil spirits, the building can be completely filled with the presence of the Lord and from the moment of consecration it is covered by His glory and protected by His power. (There is a sample dedication prayer in the appendix.)

Chapter 5

The Consecration of Land and Buildings for Worship

The current practice amongst many churches of consecrating new buildings for the use of Christian worship is one that has been in existence for many centuries and has largely remained unchanged. It is based upon the dedication and the later purification of the temple of Solomon. The first record of this service can be found in the writings of Eusebius, one of the Greek fathers of the church. Eusebius was a church historian who has been described as the "father of church history". He was born in AD 260 or 270 and became the bishop of Caesarea. This service of consecration set apart the church exclusively for the worship and praise of God and the blessing of His people.

It was never intended that the building where the Lord is worshiped should become the main focus of attention. This can lead to the sin of idolatry, which has been a weakness from the earliest times of the tabernacle in the wilderness, to our modern-day cathedrals. The Israelites were convinced that because the temple of Solomon was the dwelling place of God it would never be destroyed, even though the people were sinful (Jeremiah 7:4, 12), but of course it was destroyed (2 Kings 25:9). The sin of idolatry occurs when God's people take their eyes off the Lord and consider the temple or church where He is worshiped as more important than the Lord Himself (Luke 21:5; Mark 13:1). Idolatry can occur among Christians when anything other than the Lord becomes our main focus.

However, the fact that spiritual truth is abused does not mean that the truth itself is wrong. In seeking to bring reformation, we must be careful not to "throw the baby out with the bath water!" There is much useful spiritual understanding that God has given to the church which needs rediscovering. The consecration of a new church was never meant to imply that the living God could be contained within its walls. As far as the Old Testament is concerned the temple held a unique place in the worship of the Lord. It was the only place where the Israelites could bring their sacrifices. Also, the males had to come to the temple of the Lord in Jerusalem three times a year (Exodus 23:14, 17). It was the place from which He would hear them when they called upon Him (2 Chronicles 7:14–16).

There was an argument amongst the Jews and Samaritans over where worship should take place. For the Jews it was Jerusalem, for the Samaritans it was Mount Gerizim. When Jesus came, He told the Samaritan woman that the time had come when the place where the Father was worshiped would extend beyond a single mountain (John 4:21–24).

Solomon did not think that the temple he had built could contain the living God (2 Chronicles 2:6). There is an interesting quote from *History of the Christian Church* by Philip Schaff that gives an insight into the thinking of the early church over the issue of consecrated church buildings:

> "When Athanasius was once censured for assembling the congregation on Easter, for want of room, in a newly built but not yet consecrated church, he appealed to the injunction of the Lord, that we enter into our closet to pray, as consecrating every place. Chrysostom urged that every house should be a church, and every head of a family a spiritual shepherd, remembering the account which he must give even for his children and servants. Not walls and roof, but faith and life, constitute the church, and the advantage of prayer in the church comes not so much from a special holiness of the place, as from the Christian fellowship, the bond of love, and the prayer of the priests."

Clearly the emphasis of the early church was upon the spiritual life of the people of God rather than a building. However, the building was not to be used for any other purpose than the reason it had been built. It therefore required setting apart and dedicating to the Lord Himself.

Sometimes the spiritual practices of the founding fathers of a church or of a Christian ministry are deceptive and are bound to create spiritual problems that if not dealt with, will continue to undermine the life and witness of the work. One example of this is the practice of Freemasonry, which can affect the spiritual life of the church.

The most important criteria for the establishment of any new work for God is that He is the one who initiates and the one who builds:

> *"Unless the LORD builds the house,*
> *its builders labour in vain.*
> *Unless the LORD watches over the city,*
> *the watchmen stand guard in vain."*   (Psalm 127:1)

The consecration of a building for Christian worship may seem unnecessary to us in the light of what Jesus said to the Samaritan woman (John 4:23–24). However, in this instance Jesus was simply extending the worship of the Father beyond the confines of the temple in Jerusalem. It is common today for new churches to use a building that does not belong to them, such as a local community center that is hired for Sunday worship. The weekly activities of the center are bound to determine the spiritual atmosphere of the building. It is difficult enough to plant a new church, but if the community center is used by other groups such as the Yoga or Martial Arts club, the spiritual atmosphere will not be open or conducive to the presence of the Holy Spirit.

The biblical practice of consecrating a place for worship

The very first place of worship to be consecrated was the movable tent or tabernacle that Moses erected for the wilderness journeys (Exodus 25–40). The second was the temple of Solomon (1 Chronicles 22), which was rebuilt by King Herod following the Babylonian captivity. The third temple is the human body that the Lord dwells in by His Holy Spirit (1 Corinthians 3:16). To begin to understand the spiritual truth behind the consecration of a place of worship let us now look at the consecration of the tabernacle.

The tabernacle and all its contents are consecrated

The tabernacle was constructed from an offering that the people of Israel freely brought consisting of:

> *" ... gold, silver and bronze; blue, purple and scarlet yarn and fine linen; goat hair; rams skins dyed red and hides of sea cows; acacia wood; olive oil for the light; spices for the anointing oil and for the fragrant incense; and onyx stones and other gems ... "*
> (Exodus 25:3–7)

All these articles had been given to the Israelites by the Egyptians when they left Egypt. Exodus 40 is the record of the setting up of the tabernacle. In verses 1–7 the individual parts are joined together to make a complete structure. In verse 9 we read:

> *"Take the anointing oil and anoint the tabernacle and everything in it; consecrate it and all its furnishings, and it will be holy. Then anoint the altar of burnt offering and all its utensils; consecrate the altar, and it will be most holy. Anoint the basin and its stand and consecrate them."*

Every part of the physical structure including the tables and utensils was anointed with oil before its use. The sacred anointing oil that was used had been specially prepared according to God's instructions. It was also to be used for the anointing of Aaron and his sons, the priests, and could not be used for any other purpose (Exodus 30:22–33). Considering the ingredients in the oil, it would have given off the most beautiful aroma. This oil represented the fragrance of the Holy Spirit. The articles used in the building of the tabernacle needed to be set apart and also to be cleansed from the defilement attached to them because of their origin. They were given to the Israelites by the Egyptians, an idolatrous nation who worshiped demons and were led by an evil man who blasphemed the living God through his religion and pride. Inanimate objects can carry evil spirits as a consequence of their use as objects of worship or can carry a curse that has been applied specifically to them. Any demonic power that was attached to the articles used in the building of the tabernacle would be removed through the application of this sacred anointing oil.

Anointing with oil imparts holiness

The action of consecration and anointing not only changes the use of something or someone, but it also imparts God's holiness to it. That this characteristic of holiness was imparted to the curtains and furniture of the tabernacle can be understood when considering that whatever touched the furniture and the utensils would become holy (Exodus 30:29). This anointing oil was sacred and could not be made by any of the people nor could it be applied to men's bodies unless they were priests descended from Aaron (Exodus 30:31–33).

There is no present-day requirement for this specially formulated and sacred oil as now the Holy Spirit Himself has been poured out on the whole church and He is present with all God's people (Numbers 11:29; John 14:17). This special oil was used at a time when only the descendants of Aaron could become priests before God, but this is no longer the case (Revelation 1:6; 1 Peter 2:9). Now every genuine believer is a priest and has personal and continual access to the very presence of God through Jesus Christ the only mediator (1 Timothy 2:5).

New Testament anointing

Anointing with oil is a practice that continued all through New Testament times and down through the ages of church history. Although the oil that was used by the apostles and which we use today is different from that used by the Aaronic Priesthood in Old Testament times, the principle remains the same: to set apart or consecrate something or someone for God and for a specific purpose. The oil used by the disciples of Jesus was ordinary olive oil (Mark 6:13; James 5:14). We have already seen that when oil is used to consecrate something or someone, the thing or person anointed is touched by God's holiness. Therefore, something of God's Spirit touches and remains upon the thing or person anointed.

James 5:14 teaches that the oil is to be applied upon the body of the sick believer. Many believers can testify to the presence of the Holy Spirit coming upon them when they are anointed in this way. Concerning the Christian's physical body Scripture says:

> *"Don't you know that you yourselves are God's temple and that God's Spirit lives in you?"*
> (1 Corinthians 3:16; see also 6:19–20)

This is the third temple that God has chosen to dwell in. It is appropriate that the practice of anointing should continue for the consecration or setting apart of Christian disciples for particular service to the Lord. It became the practice of the church for the bishop to pray over the oil before it was used. The oil was then kept in the church for use by the ordained minister. This continues to be a practice of some churches to this day. Whilst this is a practice that ought to be encouraged, it is worth pointing out that the oil is no less blessed when prayed over by any genuine believer. The Scriptures encourage the people of God to seek their leaders for prayer when sick (James 5:14) but they do not restrict the ministry to the sick only to those who are leaders (Mark 16:17–18; John 14:12). The Holy Spirit dwells in every genuine believer. As a ministry, we have prayed for many sick people over the last fourteen years and have seen the Holy Spirit bring the presence of God with deep healing.

It is interesting to note that there is no reference in either the Old or New Testaments to the anointing oil being prayed over prior to its use. As far as the Old Testament is concerned it is clear that the special oil could only be used for specific purposes given by the Lord Himself. This was not the case with the olive oil used in the New Testament; nor with most oil used today. Olive oil has a variety of different uses – it can be anointed for healing or simply used for cooking. But if it is to be used for holy purposes it makes sense to pray over it. In

New Testament times we do not know for certain whether the disciples prayed over it or not, but I suspect that they did for the reason that I have given. We may think of oil as only a symbol of the Holy Spirit that has no real power in itself. However, Tom Marshall in his book *Healing from the Inside Out* says that "... in the Bible a symbol is not a substitute for the real thing; it is the means by which the real thing is communicated or mediated. The Ark of the Covenant was not a substitute for the presence of God; it was the place where God's presence was manifested."

The floor of the tabernacle

So far we have not considered the consecration of the ground itself. The tabernacle was designed to be taken down and carried to its next resting place. No floor had been constructed for the tabernacle as it was designed to rest upon the ground, which in this case happened to be the sand of the desert. The very presence of God would be the means whereby the plot of ground was consecrated just as it was consecrated in the burning bush when He appeared to Moses. God told Moses to take off his sandals. He had a similar requirement for the Aaronic priests, for there were no sandals or shoes prescribed along with the priestly garments as they were to minister barefoot in the tabernacle. Each time they entered the tabernacle for service they were to wash their hands and their feet (Exodus 30:21; 40:30–32). This ritual washing would spiritually cleanse their feet from defilement as a consequence of walking on the unholy ground outside the tabernacle.

The consecration of the temple

Like Moses, David had received specific plans for the building of the temple, although it was for his son Solomon to build it (1 Chronicles 28:10–19). King David, who had gathered treasures from the nations he had conquered, had already dedicated to God the silver and gold and all the furnishings used in the construction of the temple. The Bible doesn't say how King David dedicated these treasures but it's most likely it was done with prayer and thanksgiving (2 Samuel 8:11; 1 Kings 7:51; 2 Chronicles 5:1). It seems that the only piece of furniture that Solomon did not make was the Ark of the

Covenant. The Ark was placed in its proper resting-place in the inner sanctuary (2 Chronicles 5:7) or most holy place. The priests withdrew from the most holy place, and began with one voice to give thanks and praise to the Lord. Then the temple of the Lord was filled with a cloud, for the glory of the Lord filled the temple. The priests were overcome by the Lord's glory and had to leave the holy place. Solomon then consecrated the temple that had now become God's dwelling place and the place where God's people could worship and seek Him when in need (2 Chronicles 6:12–42).

The fire that fell that day from heaven never fell again on the temple sacrifices. It was the responsibility of the priest to keep the fire of the Lord continually burning. This fire is something that we see when the Lord sanctifies for Himself a new dwelling place (2 Chronicles 7:1). It happened at the consecration of the tabernacle when fire came down from heaven and consumed the sacrifice (Leviticus 9:23–24). It happened on the Day of Pentecost when what seemed to be tongues of fire fell from heaven upon each of the disciples. This fire signifies holiness and purity and also that the Lord is doing a new thing among His people. It indicates His acceptance of the vessels that have been prepared for His dwelling.

Chapter 6

Cleansing from Defilement and Rededication of the Temple

The cleansing of the temple in Jerusalem by King Hezekiah has become the basic pattern for the consecration of church buildings today. An understanding of these principles and their application is vital in knowing how to remove the legal right that sin has given to demonic powers and the very demons themselves.

Several kings attempted reformation of the temple and its idolatrous practices, such as King Asa (2 Chronicles 14:1–2; 15:16), King Jehosophat (2 Chronicles 17:6) and King Joash (2 Chronicles 24). However, these attempts did not go far enough (2 Chronicles 15:17). The enemy will never be driven out completely unless there is total and complete repentance including full restoration from the damaging effects of corrupt worship. There were two major occasions when the temple of Solomon was completely cleansed from defilement. One was during the reign of King Hezekiah (2 Chronicles 29:1–35), and the other during the reign of King Josiah who reigned seventy-five years later (2 Kings 23:1–30). Sadly it did not remain clean for very long. The worship of God from age to age has suffered defilement through impure worship and general lack of obedience by the people of God. Frequently there was a mixture of worship given to God and to Baal throughout the history of the Jewish nation. Modern-day Christians have committed similar sin. A mixture of truth and error, pure worship and corrupt worship can be seen in the church. We have already seen that the consequences of sin give demonic powers access not only to individual lives but also to the ground on which we live and worship. Not only do we need to recognize sin and turn away from it, but we also need to deal with sin in all its manifold consequences (James 1:15; Galatians 6:7).

Kings Ahaz and Hezekiah

King Ahaz was unfaithful to the Lord and promoted wicked-ness in the land through the sin of idolatry. He defiled the land and the temple through false worship and closed the temple, putting an end to any worship of the Lord there (2 Chronicles 28:19–25).

When Hezekiah became king, he followed the Lord's ways and cleansed the land (2 Kings 18:3–4). The second book of Chronicles gives a fuller description of all that he did. One of Hezekiah's acts as the new king was to repair the temple doors and to re-open the temple for the worship of the Lord (2 Chronicles 29:3). Before the temple could be used again for the worship of the Lord it had to be cleansed from all that had made it unclean. It required specific action to deal with the direct consequences of false worship.

Following the purification of the temple by King Hezekiah, true worship and sacrifice were restored to the daily service of the temple according to the Law of Moses. There were several important actions necessary before true worship could be restored in the temple. The first was the cleansing and con-secration of the priests themselves, secondly the removal of all defiling objects from the temple and third, the consecration of the temple itself. This was followed by the re-introduction of daily worship and service in the temple (2 Chronicles 29:5).

Step 1 The consecration of the priests
In 2 Chronicles 29:15 we read that Hezekiah instructed the Levites to gather together and consecrate themselves to the Lord before they began their work of purifying the temple. Their duties were clearly laid out in Scripture in relation to their work in the temple (1 Chronicles 23:28–31), but these sacred duties had not been practiced (2 Chronicles 29:11; Isaiah 36:7; Jeremiah 11:13). It seems that the Levites had not

stood against King Ahaz in his determination to close the temple and had not resisted his practice of building altars on the street corners of Jerusalem, which was an act of disobedience to the Law of Moses (Deuteronomy 12:11–14). The people had forsaken the Lord and turned their faces away from His dwelling place (2 Chronicles 29:6). If the people of God were to come back to the true worship of the Lord in His temple, the work had to start with those who had the responsibility for service in the temple: the Levites.

This principle still holds true today even though there is now no special category of priests within the people of God who act as mediators for the rest. Some sin issues can only be dealt with by the leadership. Leadership is a particular gift that not every believer has been given. The principle and practice of appointing and setting apart leaders is as necessary today as it was then (Ephesians 4:9–13). Leaders are not responsible for doing everything themselves, as they don't have all the practical abilities or gifts of the Holy Spirit, but they are responsible for releasing those who do have the necessary gifting, and for ensuring that the job gets done.

Leaders must ensure that the people of God are cared for, protected, and taught the Word of God (Ezekiel 34:1–6; James 3:1). Whatever their personal gifting they are an example that others will learn from and be guided by, whether good or bad. Leaders are also responsible for maintaining truth and purity amongst the people of God and they are the ones who must take the initiative in the process of restoring truth and purity where it has become defiled. Unless leaders are themselves consecrated to the Lord, they cannot hope to cleanse the work of God from defilement, nor can they restore the pure worship of the church when it has become defiled (1 Timothy 4:16).

The Levites had been negligent in their service of the Lord (2 Chronicles 29:11). Consequently, the anger of God had fallen upon His people (2 Chronicles 29:8) so that they were under the power of their enemies (2 Chronicles 29:9). Leaders who are not consecrated or vigilant are not able to care for and protect the people that they lead.

Step 2 The removal of defiling objects from the sanctuary
In 2 Chronicles 29:16 we read that the priests went into the

sanctuary and brought out everything that was unclean into the courtyard. It was later taken to the Kidron valley and destroyed by fire. The scripture here in Chronicles does not give a description of what objects were removed. However, if we turn to the later purification of the temple by King Josiah we see that what he removed were the articles used in the worship of Baal and Asherah (2 Kings 23:4, 6).

Scripture makes repeated references to the ungodly practice of erecting Asherah poles (1 Kings 14:15 and 14:23; 2 Kings 17:10), which the Israelites were expressly commanded to destroy (Exodus 34:13). The goddess Asherah was the consort of El and the chief Canaanite god. It is thought that an Asherah pole was a carved image of the goddess. Baal and Asherah poles were to be found alongside each other (Judges 6:25). These poles were normally erected on high places and under trees (1 Kings 14:23), but to add to the insult against the Lord, Asherah poles were actually brought into the temple of the Lord (2 Kings 23:4). King Josiah also removed altars built on the roof of the temple buildings (2 Kings 23:12). It is fairly certain that Hezekiah had to remove similar articles as he had to deal with years of corrupted worship (2 Chronicles 29:16). The people of God had turned away from the Lord and forsaken Him.

> *"They abandoned the temple of the LORD, the God of their fathers, and worshipped Asherah poles and idols. Because of their guilt, God's anger came upon Judah and Jerusalem."*
> (2 Chronicles 24:18)

Inanimate objects could have a demon attached to them so these objects had to be removed and then destroyed and the temple itself purified, if the presence and power of the enemy was to be removed from the temple of the Lord. The spiritual atmosphere of the temple would be highly demonized as a consequence of the presence of these occult objects, which were used in the worship of demons. It is not so much the articles themselves that were the problem but it is what they were used for – the worship of Satan. This is offensive to the Lord wherever it takes place, but it is a great sin for it to be allowed in the very temple where God Himself is worshiped, and by those who had been given the sacred task of organizing His worship. It is the spirit of demonic worship ultimately directed to Satan that defiles and corrupts the very place where it is offered. Removal of the objects does not go far enough. The use of these objects has actually opened the temple to visitation by evil spirits. In the Old Testament demons were dealt with indirectly through the application of the Law of Moses and its prescribed ritual as well as the use of anointing oil. New Testament believers have been given Christ's personal authority to cast out demons directly (Matthew 10:1; Mark 3:15; Luke 9:1; Luke 10:19; Matthew 28:18–20; Mark 16:15–18). Also included in New Testament ministry practice is the use of oil (Mark 6:13).

Idols can even be found in the homes of Christians. I visited a Christian home in North America with a large entrance hall, and the first sight that greeted my eyes on being invited to come in was a huge statue of Buddha. The owners were of Chinese origin, and expressed to me in the course of our conversation that they really wanted to serve God and to put Him first in their lives. When I mentioned the inconsistency of allowing a statue of Buddha to greet all visitors to their Christian dwelling, their response was that they must get rid of it. But the idol was too heavy for two men to lift and it was made of Jade, a very hard substance, so it could not be broken by an ordinary hammer. They suggested using the contractors who were landscaping their property who had a large hammer. Until then we would pray over it and cover it completely with a cloth. We gathered around the idol and I read from the Bible the following passage:

> *"The images of their gods you are to burn in the fire. Do not covet the silver and gold on them, and do not take it for yourselves, or you will be ensnared by it, for it is detestable to the LORD your God. Do not bring a detestable thing into your house or you, like it, will be set apart for destruction. Utterly abhor and detest it, for it is set apart for destruction."*
>
> (Deuteronomy 7:25–26)

The husband and wife invited Jesus to be Lord of their lives and their home. Then the husband confessed and repented of his sin in allowing this offence to the Lord in his house and asked for forgiveness. He then took authority over the evil spirit attached to the idol and broke the power of all curses upon him, his family, his employees and his home in the name of Jesus Christ, ordering the spirits to leave his house. We covered the idol completely, awaiting the contractors to destroy it. The peace of Jesus was now free to fill the house and not the false peace of Buddha.

It is important to understand that these idols must be destroyed. When discussing these issues with a Chinese sister in Christ, she told me of a Chinese pastor she knew who over the years collected many idols given by people who asked him to remove curses from their lives and homes. He duly prayed over the idol, broke the curse and then took the idol away and placed it in his basement! Over the years he collected many idols which filled his basement. When asked why he kept these he said that they were valuable and harmless now that the evil spirits had been cast out of them! Needless to say the man was deceived and in darkness as a consequence of his presumption. Sadly, after his death, his daughter took some of her father's idols to her home.

Step 3 *The purification of the sanctuary and all the articles*
Following the removal of these symbols of false worship the Levites purified the sanctuary itself (2 Chronicles 29:16). Whilst the scripture does not say how they did this, it is likely that they followed the practice recorded in Exodus when the tabernacle itself was anointed (Exodus 40:9). The very walls and floor of the holy place needed re-consecrating to the Lord as the objects of Baal worship had been placed within them. Thus the defiling presence of unclean spirits had been given access to the temple of God. All of the utensils and furniture were defiled also.

> *"Then they went in to King Hezekiah and reported: 'We have purified the entire temple of the* Lord*, the altar of burnt offering with all its utensils, and the table for setting out the consecrated bread, with all its articles.'"*   (2 Chronicles 29:18)

They purified what was in the temple and brought back and

consecrated all the articles that King Ahaz had removed from the temple (2 Chronicles 29:19; 2 Chronicles 28:21). The need for purification of all these articles arises not only from the collection of dust or dirt, or even that they had been put to common use, but that they had become defiled through contact with the unclean spirits associated with idol worship.

Step 4 Reintroduction of blood sacrifices
Second Chronicles 29:20–24 records that the next act of consecration was the offering of the sacrifices prescribed according to the Law of Moses. There was no other ground upon which the living God could be approached for worship except by the shedding of blood, as there was no other way that the people could have their sins atoned for (Hebrews 9:22; Leviticus 17:11).

Today, when Christians practice evil and turn away from the true worship of the living God, the Holy Spirit brings us back to the sacrifice of the Son of God who died for our sins and was raised for our justification (Romans 4:25). Any present-day work of restoration will need to start with confession and repentance from sin, as well as faith in the finished work of Christ on the cross. In fact if the atonement of Jesus is not the foundation of our worship and service for the Lord, then we are in the flesh, and can never please the Lord (Romans 8:8). Operating in the flesh always gives evil spirits power over us and in us (Galatians 5:19–21; Ephesians 4:27). Furthermore, any spiritual experience or power that bypasses the cross is unlikely to be the Holy Spirit, but a counterfeit spirit, or in other words, a demon!

Step 5 Reintroduction of praise and worship
It is right to praise the Lord for He requires our worship. God has given us the ten commandments in order to keep the worship of the living God pure and to protect His people from idolatry, which opens us up to demonization. It is natural for the child of God to express thanks and devotion to the Lord through words accompanied by musical instruments. For a long time the temple was empty of the sound of praise. Even today Satan tries all he can to extinguish praise from the

mouths of believers whose bodies are temples of the living God.

Hezekiah instructed the Levites to praise the Lord with musical instruments in the way King David had taught (2 Chronicles 20:25–26). Why didn't King Hezekiah start the process of consecrating the temple with praise and worship? May I suggest that the reason he did not was that the priests had not yet consecrated themselves and neither had they removed from the temple the things that were an offence to God? We cannot assume that our praise and worship is acceptable to God unless we have first dealt with sin, which involves not only repentance but also the removal of that which is offensive to the Lord. After the Levites began their beautiful worship of God the whole congregation joined in (2 Chronicles 29:28).

Step 6 Reintroduction of freewill giving

The people of God were so moved and excited by all that had taken place that they now wanted to give personal offerings to the Lord (2 Chronicles 29:31–34). The priests were overwhelmed by all that the people were bringing. The hearts of the people of Israel were overflowing with all God's forgiveness and blessings upon them. After only sixteen days of cleansing the temple, the service of the temple of the Lord was re-established and the people rejoiced (2 Chronicles 29:17 and 36).

A glad heart is a direct outworking of a right relationship with God and is a necessary requirement for true giving that is acceptable to the Lord (2 Corinthians 9:7). Jesus said that those who had been forgiven much would love much, and one of the ways that love is expressed is through giving (Luke 7:47).

Step 7 Reintroduction of the Passover

The next thing Hezekiah did was to invite the whole of Israel from Beersheba to Dan to celebrate the Passover feast at the temple in Jerusalem (2 Chronicles 30). This was the first time since the Assyrian captivity that it was possible for all Israel to be together for this most important feast. When the people of God put God at the center of their lives He brought blessings and joy upon them (2 Chronicles 30:27). The modern-day application of this step is to return to a Christianity that is based upon the atoning sacrifice of Christ, our Passover Lamb (1 Corinthians 5:7), the recognition of the Lordship of Jesus over His Church (Colossians 1:18), and the unity of all believers (Psalm 133).

Finally, the cleansing of the land

The towns, which had become unclean through the erection of altars to demon gods were now cleansed, the Asherah poles cut down and the high places destroyed (2 Chronicles 31:1). The cleansing started at the temple of God and not until everything that was offensive to God was destroyed, was the work considered to be finished and the people were free to return home.

We see this practice of destroying occult objects in the New Testament. It occurs as a direct response to the proclamation of the gospel to signify allegiance to Christ and submission to His Lordship. It is an outworking of repentance from a conviction of sin and guilt.

> *"Many of those who believed now came and openly confessed their evil deeds. A number who had practised sorcery brought their scrolls together and burned them publicly. When they calculated the value of the scrolls, the total came to fifty thousand drachmas. In this way the word of the Lord spread widely and grew in power."* (Acts 19:18–20)

Ellel Ministries has conducted many conferences across the world where people have been encouraged to bring their occult objects for destruction. The result of this is that the powers of darkness lose their hold over the hearts and minds of God's people and the people themselves get healed, sometimes instantaneously. From the rise of the occult at the turn of the twentieth century to the present day, the world has been made increasingly unclean by the presence of many occult objects. We shall not see this uncleanness completely removed until Jesus Christ the Son of God comes again and ushers in the millennial reign that will eventually lead to a new heaven and a new earth wherein righteousness dwells.

Chapter 7

How Churches and Christian Structures Become Defiled

In this chapter we shall consider various activities that will allow demonic powers access to church buildings. Today many churches are purposefully desecrated – with anything from mindless acts of vandalism to Satanic acts with a clear intention to defile.

It might surprise some when I say that churches can be infiltrated by demons through the church members. This can happen through the practice of sin, which no Christian is yet free from. The big problem here is that sin in the church is often swept under the carpet and therefore the spiritual consequences are never dealt with. Anything that is hidden can be used by the enemy. It is not until issues are brought into the light that God can deal with them. Basic to our effectiveness in dealing with spiritual defilement is an understanding of the opening that sin gives to demons and how they can use this as an opportunity to attack us. It is vital that we walk in the light by dealing with sin if we are to overcome the powers of darkness and take the enemy's ground from beneath him, removing his presence (James 4:7; 2 Corinthians 2:11; Luke 10:19).

The following understanding is based on years of extensive experience in personal deliverance and also of the spiritual cleansing and deliverance of buildings.

The prior use of the land

When considering the following activities it is important to bear in mind the prior use of the land, and its former buildings, as well as the uses of the building before it became a church. Only then will we know what we are dealing with. Some of the information that we need may not be recorded. We shall therefore need revelation from the Lord Himself. Such revelation must always be tested by several mature Christians, and must include the leadership of the church (1 Thessalonians 5:21; 1 John 4:1).

Occultism

The word 'occult' means something that is hidden or supernatural like witchcraft or something that is magic or mysterious. Many Christians know that it is dangerous to be involved in occult activity. However, there are differences of opinion among Christians as to what actually constitutes occult activity, and what the consequences of that activity may be. This should not surprise us as we are dealing here with deception from the realm of darkness. Whilst these days there is much openness to occult practice, the real dangers are still hidden. The following is a list of some occult activities that can occur in a building used by a church such as a church hall. Furthermore, participation in these activities by church members outside of the premises can also give the enemy an opening to the church.

- *Fortune-telling or divination.* This may occur during a church fair, the objective being to raise money for the church. A church member dresses up like a gypsy and tells fortunes with the use of a glass ball or by reading palms. We cannot expect to escape the consequences of fooling around with these activities even though it may be done in fun. God will be displeased, and Satan will take it as a serious invitation (Leviticus 19:26; Deuteronomy 18:10–12). The use of ouija boards is also a forbidden practice.

- *Halloween parties.* Someone may dress up as the devil for a bit of harmless fun! Whilst this may seem hilarious, it can open the church to spirits of confusion, deception, or possibly worse.

- *Yoga classes.* Usually these take place in order to connect with the community by providing something that is seen to be beneficial to people. Yoga postures are designed to worship Hindu gods and so are likely to invite spirits of Hinduism into the church.

- *Martial Arts Clubs.* The practice of Martial Arts opens churches up to religious spirits of Shintoism, Taoism, Confucianism, and spirits of violence, murder and death. This is true for the hard styles of the Martial Arts such as Karate as well as the soft styles such as Ta'i Chi.

- *Spiritualist groups.* It may be that a Spiritualist group needs somewhere to "worship" and they may ask permission to use a Christian church. Spiritualism is forbidden by Scripture (Leviticus 19:31). Scripture teaches that its practice brings defilement. The punishment for its practice under the law was death (1 Chronicles 10:13). The Lord said that He would set His face against the person who practiced Spiritism (Leviticus 20:6). One could hardly expect the atmosphere to be unaffected by such practices. Bear in mind that these practices may have taken place during the time of previous occupants or in the history of the church.

- *New Age.* New Age spirits can be introduced into the church by allowing some alternative therapy groups to use church premises for practices such as acupuncture, aromatherapy, reflexology and homeopathy (2 Corinthians 11:14; Revelation 12:9; Acts 8:9–11; 1 John 2:26). Sometimes church members can participate in these things through ignorance of the spiritual dangers.

The effect of these practices, whether they are conducted in the church or in the private lives of the members, will be to undermine the spiritual life of the church, especially in the areas of committed discipleship, worship and the practice of spiritual gifts.

Other religious faiths

Ecumenical projects where Christians from different Christian denominations share the same building is perhaps a welcome practice although it is not without its problems. A problem could arise if any of these Christian groups are in serious error, or they fail to deal with the sins of their members. However, the use of Christian buildings by Hindus, Moslems, Sikhs, and other religious faiths will open the buildings to the religious spirit of that particular religion. This will happen even though the Christian congregation does not meet or join in with the other religions in their services. What is being offered, and by the leadership, is a direct invitation to the demonic power behind the false faith. The enemy will take full advantage of this clear and personal invitation coming as it does with the agreement of the Christian shepherd of the flock. What this does is to open the door of the church for the religious spirit. Its presence will stifle worship.

Sexual sin

Sexual sin of all kinds may happen on church premises including child sexual abuse. It is a sad but true fact today that sexual sin is a major problem in the body of Christ, even among church leaders. The sons of Eli are an example of sexual sin among leaders. They had sex with the women who served the tabernacle (1 Samuel 2:22–26). Hophni and Phinehas were put to death for this and other sins (1 Samuel 2:34; 4:11). Not only were the two sons judged but so too was Eli for allowing his sons to continue in their wickedness. The Lord took the priesthood from his family as a consequence (1 Samuel 2:27–36).

Sexual sin in the leader is a serious problem, as it opens both him and his church to unclean spirits. Adultery, pornography, and sexual abuse are prime examples of common sexual sins, particularly among men. A church which has as its leader someone who is in adultery, is a church that is likely to have all kinds of sexual problems among its members, including breakdown in marriage, and even abortion as a consequence of sexual sin. This will open the church to spirits of death also. The consequences of sexual sin need dealing with if the church is to be cleansed from darkness (procedures for doing this are in chapter 9).

Today there is the ever-present problem of pedophiles. The Lord Jesus loves all sinners and His grace is sufficient to forgive their sin, but the church needs protecting. Such men can have held office in the church for years as Sunday school teachers or youth leaders, without anyone suspecting a thing, although sometimes knowledge of their sins is very public. This is a serious matter if no one knows they are present and is therefore not checking on their behavior, as children can be at serious risk. Although previous offenders may not have given in to their unclean and perverted desires, it is unlikely that any personal ministry has been offered even when the problem has been known about. Of course people with such problems should not be allowed to have anything to do with children, and the laws in many countries forbid it.

Blessing or cursing?

There are specific consequences that will follow disobedience. This is not something that we can relegate to Old Testament times. Leviticus 26, Deuteronomy 27 and 28 list the rewards for obedience and punishments/curses for disobedience. These curses are just as likely to fall on believers of the new covenant as they were on believers in the old covenant. The curses that Christians need deliverance from may have been affecting the individual long before they came to faith in Christ, but because of lack of understanding the curses have not been dealt with.

Although the curses mentioned in Deuteronomy 27 and 28 were spoken specifically to the Hebrew nation, we as God's new covenant people may well be affected by such curses. Jesus Christ through His death and resurrection has broken the curse of the law, and through Him we can be delivered from any curses affecting us (Galatians 3:13). However, there must be an application of the work of Christ to the sin which needs not only specific confession, but also healing (1 John 1:8–9; James 5:13–16). Many stop with repentance and do not proceed to seek deliverance from the power of the enemy and healing from any sickness that has been visited upon them.

There are always consequences for disobeying God's Word (James 1:15). On what biblical grounds do we think that as New Testament believers we can receive blessings and be protected from curses? It is a deception to think that we can sin without there being any consequences (Galatians 6:7). And it is spiritual blindness not to discern the presence of demons (2 Corinthians 2:11). Although Galatians 6:7 does not explicitly teach the consequences of each sin, it does teach that there will be reaping in accordance with the sin that is sown. We need to remember that the Old Testament Scriptures were known and understood by the Galatians who received Paul's letter and that they understood the specific consequences of the sins of idolatry and immorality.

Sins of the leaders

The sins of leaders will always give the enemy opportunities to get at the children of God. God has given leaders His authority to protect and deal with the enemy's attack against the people of God. A good pastor will be like a shepherd to the sheep or a gate to his church. He has been given authority to drive away the enemy and to guide the people of God. He can be described like Jesus as, "the gate for the sheep" (John 10:7). If the enemy is to be effective he must get past the leader which he will seek to do by leading the pastor into personal sin or by trying to keep him in darkness and even deception over areas of truth (Hebrews 3:13; 1 Corinthians 6:9; 1 Timothy 4:16).

Sometimes Christian leaders fall into moral sins and at other times are guilty of wrong teaching, bringing deception followed by destruction into the church. It is always sad when this happens as it gives Satan an opportunity to destroy the individual leader and the church or ministry that they are involved with.

Jim Bakker is an example of a fall caused by wrong teaching which, tragically for him, led to a prison sentence. Goodness knows how many Christians were deceived by his wrong teaching. Jim Bakker was a very successful leader who was the host of the American PTL television show and the head of an empire encompassing Heritage USA and the Inspirational Network. He taught that God wanted to bless His children with wealth and became associated with what has come to be known as "prosperity teaching". He was accused of fraud, tried and convicted, and given a 45-year prison sentence! The Lord helped him and he was released from prison after serving much less than his original sentence. As a consequence of all that he experienced he is a wiser man. He wrote a book in which he penned the following words:

> "As the true impact of Jesus' words regarding money impacted my heart and mind, I became physically nauseated. I was wrong! I was wrong in my lifestyle, certainly, but even more fundamentally wrong in my understanding of the Bible's message. Not only was I wrong, but I was teaching the opposite of what Jesus had said!"
>
> (From *I Was Wrong*, Thomas Nelson Publishers)

I was deeply challenged as I considered God's dealing with this leader and encouraged by the grace of God that he was able to grasp, leading to his forgiveness and repentance. Sadly, not all fallen leaders allow the Lord to produce in them such depth of repentance and restoration. Many still continue in their deception.

Some other deceptions of leaders

Freemasonry

The practice of Freemasonry by church leaders will open the church to demonic powers. In the first three degrees of Freemasonry, oaths are taken using different names for God not found in the Bible. Freemasons are taught initially that the name for God is "the Great Architect of the Universe" (TGAOTU). In the further degrees, such as the so-called "Holy Royal Arch" degree, the oath is taken in the "sacred name" Jah Bul On. Jah is a corruption of Jehovah or Yahweh; the revealed name of God, Bul is derived from Baal, and On is derived from Osiris, the Egyptian god of the dead. Freemasons are taught in the 32nd degree that the name of God is Ahura-Masda. In North American Freemasonry there is an order called "Shriners" in which the oaths are taken in the name of Allah. To associate the name of God with idols is blasphemous. Finally, Freemasons learn that the name of God is none other than Lucifer!

American Shriners wear a red Fez hat on their head; this is a brimless felt cap with a flat top and tassel worn by men in some Muslim countries. It is not generally known that this is a symbol of the "defeat of Christianity" as the red color comes from being dipped in the blood of Christians shed by Muslims. The famous British comedian Tommy Cooper used to wear such a hat for his comedy routines!

The spirit of Anti-Christ is behind this deception, but there are many other spirits such as curses of death and sickness as well as curses on the finances and the spiritual life of the church. Many churches have founding fathers who were Freemasons. For a fuller understanding of Freemasonry see *Freemasonry and Christianity. Are they Compatible?* by Church House Publishing ISBN 0 7151 37166.

Domination and manipulation

This is not a sin confined only to church leaders but if the leader is a controlling person then the Spirit of the Lord will be hindered in the life of the church. The history of churches and Christian movements verifies that this sin is common among leaders.

I remember an occasion when, with my fellow prayer minister, we saw a woman delivered from a spirit of control that she had received as a consequence of membership of her church. She was a member no longer, but she continued the practice of wearing a head covering. She wore this at the first meeting of the healing retreat and noticed that she was the only woman to do so. She decided not to wear it the following day. She felt fearful and mentioned this to us. We asked her why she wore it and this was her reason. When she visited her former church for the first time a lady next to her had opened her handbag and offered her a headscarf. "There you are dear," she said, "you can give it back to me when you buy one for yourself." She did just this and also bought an extra one just in case she ever sat next to a new visitor like herself. Every woman in this church wears a head covering because the pastor insists upon it! Now whatever you may think about this subject is not the issue here. The issue is that there is outright pressure from the pastor for all women, irrespective of their beliefs and feelings over the matter, to wear a head covering. This has the effect of overriding the conscience and free will of the individual, and constitutes control. The enemy will always ride in on this kind of control.

People who are controlled in various ways will be crushed and made vulnerable to all kinds of deception. Perhaps all of us are guilty of the sin of trying to control others in an ungodly way from time to time. I know I have been guilty of this sin. It is a major problem if it is firmly and deeply established in the heart of the leader, as he/she will not be able to recognize this sin easily even when others point it out. It is a real test of character for a leader to be willing to face issues like these.

Although there are many accusations of control leveled against leaders, not all are true. They sometimes come from hurting people who have been abused and have decided never to trust anyone in authority. They may also come from Christians who are not willing to submit to godly authority and discipline. The accusation of control, indeed any sin against a leader, needs confirming by at least two or three people (1 Timothy 5:19). Often these accusations are made behind someone's back so there is no possibility of dealing with them.

False teaching
We all like to think that our teaching is biblical and therefore the truth. However, if we are to be honest, those of us who preach and teach may have shared teaching at some time in our ministry that we now recognize as being error. Perhaps the most common area for error is in the work of the Holy Spirit and spiritual gifts. I have repented over the fact that for years I made people suspicious of spiritual gifts, especially the gift of tongues. I thought I had the truth, but the Holy Spirit convicted me that I was wrong. I was taught dispensational theology as a young Christian. Dispensational theology teaches what some have called the "cessationist view". This is the belief that the sign-gifts such as tongues and healing, including deliverance, were only to authenticate the ministry of the apostles until the canon of the New Testament was completed.

I was involved in a lively church for seven years as its associate pastor. I was told by one of the leaders with knowledge of the history of the church, that the founding pastor, who was a godly man, had said, "No one in this church will ever speak in tongues." To this day I believe no one ever has, at least publicly. There was once a leader within the church who did receive the gift of tongues but he resigned his membership!

Through wrong agreements

An agreement is only rarely a formal document which both parties sign. It more often means walking together in some aspect of life, either in harmony or for a common purpose, with another person or party. As Christians we can be walking in either godly or ungodly agreement with others. Godly agreement leads to fellowship, ungodly agreement leads to bondage. A godly agreement leaves the parties open to receive spiritual blessing from the Holy Spirit (Matthew 18:19–20). An ungodly agreement leaves the parties vulnerable to demonic bondage. When, in the church, we enter into agreements which open the door to demons, we are opening up the church to deception. Too often we only see agreements with our natural eyes; we fail to see the spiritual consequences, which are usually much more serious (2 John 4–11). Conversely, when we disagree with those who are being led by the Holy Spirit then we are in danger of grieving the Holy Spirit by bringing division into the body of Christ.[1]

Possible consequences of wrong agreements

We can be deceived into being involved in courses of action which are ungodly. We may be in danger of being tied in an ungodly way to those we are in a wrong agreement with. We could then become subject to the control of powers that are operating through that individual.

Deceptions taught in the Church which can potentially open the door to demonic activity

- Denial of the Virgin birth of Christ
- Denial of the sinlessness of Christ

[1] Attributed to Peter Horrobin, *Healing Through Deliverance* published by Sovereign World, 2008.

- Denial of the physical bodily resurrection of Christ
- Denial of the reality of a personal devil
- Christians cannot have a demon
- The gifts of the Spirit are not for today
- If you do not speak in tongues you have not been baptized in the Holy Spirit
- All religions will lead you to God, as all religious faiths worship the same God
- A loving God will not allow people to endure eternal punishment in hell
- A decision for Christ is sufficient to guarantee eternal salvation irrespective of lifestyle
- We do not need healing from the past when we become Christians
- God wants me to be financially rich. This teaching is sometimes called "prosperity teaching"
- Healing is my right, all I have to do is to claim it from God
- Modern medicine has replaced the healing ministry, in these days God uses only doctors and medicine
- If healing does not happen immediately it cannot be the healing ministry of Jesus
- All prophecy, healing and demonstrations of super-natural signs must be of God especially if they happen in a Christian meeting
- New Age and pseudo religious practices such as Free-masonry are harmless
- God is my covering, therefore I do not need to be accountable to anyone else
- Sexual relationships outside of marriage are acceptable provided that the two partners love each other
- The practice of homosexuality and lesbianism is accept-able behavior between loving and consenting partners
- There are no consequences for new covenant believers from the sins of their ancestors

- Any experience of love, peace and unity must come from the Holy Spirit

- We can have the power of the Holy Spirit without repentance from personal sin

- When seeking to move in the power of the Holy Spirit, the Bible isn't necessary

Exercising wrong authority

Tom Marshall in his book *Understanding Leadership*, published by Sovereign World International, reminds us that, " ... Because authority is delegated power, it can be used only by those who are in obedient relationship to the source of that power". Thus the leader's personal walk with Jesus is the vital element in the effective exercise of authority. The moment we are out of the Spirit we are in the flesh and we will be exercising fleshly or soul power. Tom Marshall goes on to say that the kind of authority exercised depends on the situation. There are three kinds of authority: task authority, teaching authority, and ethical or spiritual authority.

Task authority is to be used in situations that require some task accomplishing. The leader gives the instructions and those given the task obey and the job is done.

Teaching authority is required where Christians are learning to understand truth and how to live the Christian life. Instructions that are merely to be followed without question are inappropriate for this kind of situation. If others are to learn they must be allowed to question and discuss what is being taught. The teacher must explain the reasons for what is being said and exercise love and patience with the hearers, especially with those who do not understand at first. They must not be told to believe something merely because the teacher has said it (Acts 17:11).

Spiritual authority is needed in situations where moral guidance is being given to believers, or where they are being encouraged to be more like Jesus and are challenged over ungodly behavior. This kind of authority must not be manipulative or controlling in order to force Christians into an accepted behavior pattern, even if that behavior is biblical. Every person needs time to process new truth and must first understand it before bringing their will into line with that particular truth. The truth must register in their conscience so that there is heart-obedience to it and not only outward conformity. If we confuse the kind of authority that each situation demands we shall in effect be abusing our God-given authority and also abusing the person over whom we exercise wrong authority.

Chapter 8

How to Discern
the Presence of Evil

How can you know if evil spirits are present in a home, a church or attached to the land?

When visiting a church to teach and minister healing and deliverance one soon becomes aware of the spiritual atmosphere. Peter Horrobin, the leader of Ellel Ministries, tells of entering a church building in Sweden and recognizing immediately that something was wrong. He said to the organizer that something from the past was not dealt with. The organizer of the conference knew that the church was not growing as it ought to. The youth leaders said that they had come so far, but couldn't go further, and didn't know why, and there was also conflict in the church leadership.

Spiritual discernment is often the first step to discovering that there are issues that the church must deal with, and this is normally confirmed when the spiritual problems of the church are known. The next step is to ask the Lord to expose any spiritual darkness. One member of the visiting team discerned that there were sexual spirits in the building; another was given a picture of clowns. A lady known to the organizer, who was a conference delegate and had never been to the church before, had a vision of ugly sexual things happening on the platform, which seemed to confirm that there were sexual spirits in the building.

The Lord will often help us to understand the problem by doing a little research on the history of the area and the building. The organizer went to the local library to do some research on the history of the building and its former use. She saw some pictures that showed that the building had strong Masonic foundations and had been a music hall and brothel some one hundred years ago. No wonder then that there were Freemasonry and sexual spirits in the building! Clearly, these were the issues from the past that had not been dealt with. With the help of the team, the church leadership began the process of cleansing and delivering the land and the building. Although there are still problems, the church is beginning to experience spiritual breakthroughs and God is doing wonderful things.

I wonder how many frustrated leaders are struggling because they are affected by issues from the past?

Let us consider another example that illustrates how one can know if there is evil present. Before a Christian conference takes place it is necessary to pray throughout the building and rooms that are being rented. Major conference centers are used for all manner of gatherings from pop concerts to party political conventions, including New Age activities. A few years ago I was part of the prayer team that was praying throughout a major conference center in the South of England before its use by Ellel Ministries. Four of us went to pray in a room behind the main platform that was used by the performers and speakers, prior to their coming onto the platform or the stage. We were inviting the presence of the Lord into the room, which seemed a little heavy to me.

We prayed in the various parts of the room and after just a few minutes a young woman who was part of the team left the room quickly in tears saying as she went out that she couldn't stand being in this room any longer. The other woman in the team went after her to see what was wrong. Just then a man, who was also in the room said, "I will have to get out as well." Before he left he told me that he could sense the presence of sexual spirits. Now I knew this dear man had been sexually abused in his childhood and also that he was still in the process of receiving ministry. I did not know anything about the young woman who had left the room, but I found out later that she had also been sexually abused.

It was now clear that the heaviness that we had sensed as we went into the room was there because of the presence of sexual spirits. The man and the woman had reacted in the way that they had because they themselves were not completely healed from their abuse. This raises the question as to how these evil spirits got into this room. The likelihood is that sexual sin had been committed in the room, possibly during a pop concert when young girls are invited to meet the star afterwards. Those of us who remained in the room continued the work until the atmosphere changed. This was evidenced by the fact that the man and the woman were able to return to the room after prayer without any of the distressing feelings they had experienced before.

Those who have been specifically affected in this way are likely to be sensitive to the presence of sexual spirits. There is likely to be a special sensitivity to the presence of evil spirits when they are connected to our own pain, although the reaction will not always be as strong as in this instance, especially when healing has taken place.

However, it is not necessary to have been abused to sense the presence of sexual spirits or any other kind of evil spirit for that matter. There is a gift of discernment from the Holy Spirit that the Lord Jesus is willing to give to those who ask Him:

> *"To one there is given through the Spirit the message of wisdom, to another the message of knowledge by means of the same Spirit, to another faith by the same Spirit, to another gifts of healing by that one Spirit, to another miraculous powers, to another prophecy, to another distinguishing between spirits."*   (1 Corinthians 12:8–10)

Like any gift from the Holy Spirit it is given for a particular reason, and when needed, not only to bless the individual. Spiritual gifts can be described in different ways, and one way is as "tools for the job". If we are not doing the job then we don't need the tools! Within a church there are usually people who can exercise this gift more than others (1 Corinthians 12:10). These people need to be identified and encouraged by the leadership. This gift enables the individual to discern the presence of evil either through receiving a very strong impression that a particular evil spirit is present or by seeing a picture of something that happened in the past. This is a necessary gift if we are to be effective in dealing with demonic presence in buildings and other places. The Lord knows what needs to be dealt with and He is the revealer of secrets (Daniel 2:47; Hebrews 4:13; 1 John 3:8).

I distinctly remember being at a prayer conference, manning the Ellel Ministries stand with a colleague, when a lady who was manning a Christian stand next to ours returned from one of the meetings. She looked a little shocked, and I asked if she was all right. She told me that she had just been involved in a prayer triplet with a well known evangelist who has a well-established ministry in the area of words of knowledge. After the initial introductions he had asked her if he could share something that the Lord had shown him concerning her. She agreed, and he told her that she had a snake wrapped around her leg and that it was a spirit of witchcraft that had been in her family for generations. Would she like him to cast it out for her? She agreed, and of course the evangelist did precisely that. He was spot-on, and as you can imagine she was just a little surprised by all this, but I was able to reassure her with some more explanation, which she clearly accepted.

However, I wish to issue a word of caution here. Some of God's people who exercise this kind of gifting can be wrong or even operating out of an occult spirit without knowing it. It is important that every "revelation" is tested (1 Thessalonians 5:19–21; 1 John 4:1). It is also important to know the spiritual background of those who will form the prayer team. For instance, have they been involved in occult practices such as Spiritualism, where they may have been a medium? Or have they been involved in New Age practices, such as astral travel – an out of body experience that enables travel in the spiritual realms? Astral travel is accomplished by demonic power and can only happen when the seal holding spirit and soul together in the body is broken. And most importantly, have they been delivered of their demons (Ephesians 4:26–27)? If not, they can, as believers, be operating out of both Holy Spirit discernment and demonic discernment.

Teamwork is essential in discerning and dealing with the presence of evil spirits, but what spiritual qualities should you look for in bringing your team together? Many Christian leaders have discovered that whatever problems their church has, these problems are unlikely to improve if they allow those who are not spiritually mature to be part of the team!

The enemy would love to have people with occult gifts be released by their leaders into this ministry, as without the necessary deliverance they will inadvertently give rights to occult spirits to invade the church. Just imagine the spiritual confusion this can cause! If prayer for cleansing is begun on false information, then not only will confusion result, but also deception will enter the church, and its latter state will be worse than its former state. Below is a list of qualities to look for in choosing a prayer ministry team for service in the local church. The list also includes negative characteristics that if not dealt with would undermine the work of the Holy Spirit.

Positive characteristics to look for in choosing a prayer team

- Those who are moving in God's overall vision for their church (Nehemiah 2:17–18; Acts 16:10)
- Those who are pilgrims not settlers
- Those who want God's will more than anything else (Matthew 6:10, 33)
- Those who are in godly submission to their leadership (Hebrews 13:7 and 17)
- Those who have compassion for the sick (Matthew 9:36; Matthew 8:2; 2 Corinthians 1:3)
- Those who are willing to lay down their lives for others (John 12:24–26; Philippians 1:21)
- Those who are willing to give God the glory for what He does through them (1 Corinthians 10:31)
- Those who are busy but have time! (1 Kings 19:20)
- Those who are willing to learn (John 14:12)
- Those who are single-minded (Hebrews 12:2; Luke 9:62)
- Those who have good wholesome relationships (1 Timothy 5:1–2; Matthew 19:6)
- Those who are spiritual (Galatians 6:1)

- Those who give and command respect (1 Peter 2:17; Proverbs 11:16; 1 Thessalonians 4:12)

Negative characteristics to watch out for when choosing a prayer team

- Those who are judgmental (Matthew 7:1–2)
- Those who are harsh and critical (Ezekiel 34:4)
- Those with an unruly tongue (James 3:6–12)
- Those who are busybodies and gossips (1 Thessalonians 4:11)
- Those who are argumentative (2 Timothy 2:24–26; Titus 3:9)
- Those who are seeking status (3 John 9)
- Those who are unwilling to receive personal ministry (John 3:20; 5:40)
- Those who cannot take correction (2 Timothy 3:16; James 1:22)
- Those who panic easily (2 Timothy 4:5)
- Those who are exercising any form of ungodly control (Romans 8:8)
- Those who are independent of others (Romans 12:3–8)
- Those who are uncommitted to their local church (Hebrews 10:25)

Occasional sin in these areas will not disqualify a person from joining a ministry team. However, where there is a lifestyle characterized by such sins, then these should be dealt with first before releasing that person to minister God's love and power into the lives of others. Do not be in a rush to appoint people (1 Timothy 5:22). You may regret it later! Don't allow the need for action to push you into the wrong action. Take counsel, and go to prayer. Many works for God fail because the wrong people are chosen for the task.

A knowledge of the prior use of the land

It is essential to have a basic understanding of how demons

gain a foothold in a place, as this understanding will often give an indication of what might be present. When this knowledge is combined with knowledge of the history of the land, the building or the work carried out there, you will have a lot of the information that you need to begin the work of deliverance from evil spirits. This information can be gleaned from talking to people or by reading the records of leadership and church meetings. Obviously not everyone can do this as not everyone has access to these records. It is, of course, essential to have leadership involved in this process. A history of the land can often be gleaned from the local public library by reading newspapers and local history books.

Key points of significance to watch out for in and around church buildings are accidents, violent deaths, murders, suicides, war, execution sites, occult worship sites, hospital sites, burial sites, and slavery markets. Knowledge of who owned the land is also significant, especially if they were known to have been involved in a practice or lifestyle opposed to Christianity. Researching histories of famines, bankruptcies, and the use of buildings prior to use for Christian worship can point to deliverance needs. For example a church that now occupies a building that was formerly used by the local rugby club. One would expect to find that a building used for such purposes, where there is a likelihood of heavy drinking with its associated activities, would present one or two spiritual problems!

A history of the spiritual life in the building

When leaders sense a resistance to the freedom of the Holy Spirit, it should always be checked out. The enemy will try to hide his presence and the temptation will be to rationalize the problem by putting it down to natural causes.

A church leader told me that his church was having difficulty moving in spiritual gifts. The leadership had had a shift in theology and was looking to be open to the Holy Spirit's leading in their services. However to their surprise nothing was happening. I discovered that they had recently moved into a new building. Previously, the building had been used by a church which rejected the use of spiritual gifts such as tongues, prophecy and healing.

There are many sins in the life of a church that grieve and quench the Holy Spirit (Ephesians 4:29–32). These sins need addressing with respect to their consequences; otherwise the Holy Spirit's work will be hindered. The Bible teaches that we reap what we sow (Galatians 6:7). If we are not walking in the light we are open to darkness. If we are not walking in the truth we are open to deception. Wherever deception is present it will almost certainly give demonic powers a right to undermine the work of the Holy Spirit in the specific area of error. We must repent of all wrong teaching given on the person and work of the Holy Spirit; otherwise the exercise of spiritual gifts will be hindered or even corrupted. The course of action that one should follow in these circumstances is to repent of personal sin, to forgive one's fellow Christians for their unbelief and wrong teaching in this matter, and then to drive out the presence of the enemy.

Circumstances in church life that may indicate the need for cleansing and deliverance

The enemy is often able to attack churches and individual believers without arousing a suspicion of his presence because of a lack of understanding among Christians. This is why the first chapter of this book examines what the Bible teaches concerning the power of Satan to inflict damage upon believers. Knowledge of how Christians can be demonized is basic to understanding how they can gain access to churches. The following is a list of some circumstances that will need investigating by the leadership in order to discover and deal with the presence of demons.

Outbreaks of sickness

Particularly when several people are affected by the same illness. An example of this is ME (Myalgic Encephalitis), called Post Viral Syndrome in North America. Discussion with those who have been involved in occult practices such as Satanism and witchcraft confirms that covens perform specific rituals in order to curse Christians with sickness by sending evil spirits against them. So it is important to be aware of local covens. A characteristic that can sometimes be observed is that people who are in close fellowship with each other may be affected by the same condition. Occasionally it is the case that there is an ungodly agreement between the people in the group. For example, if the church leader is walking in the flesh in some area of his/her life it is possible that those who are close to the leader may have the same condition (Proverbs 22:24–25; Galatians 2:11–13).

Breakdown in relationships

This can be a simple falling out at one end of the scale or divorce at the other end of the scale. Witchcraft curses are one source of marital breakdown. Of course these spirits would have no power over us if we were walking in the light with the Lord and each other (Proverbs 26:2; 1 John 1:7). Only Jesus could say that the devil had no hold over Him as there was no sin in His life (John 14:30). In reality the church is full of sinful people who don't always want to deal with their sin issues. It is sometimes the case that there are people in the church who do not speak to each other and haven't done so for a long time. This is a sin that needs to be dealt with or the church will be open to visitation by demonic spirits that will promote further unforgiveness and bitterness in the congregation. This sin grieves the Holy Spirit and will rob the church of the sweet presence of God (Ephesians 4:29–32). The spirit of division is waiting to work in a believer in order to divide the church (Mark 3:24).

Sins of the tongue

Often associated with breakdown in relationship is the wrong use of the tongue. Proverbs 18:21 tells us that the power of life and death is in the tongue. This means exactly what it says, that our words will either impart life or death. This is further supported by the teaching in James 3 which says that the tongue can be *"set on fire by hell"* (James 3:6), and that among Christians the same tongue can speak praise to God and cursing to men (James 3:6–10).

> *"Out of the same mouth come praise and cursing. My brothers,*
> *this should not be."*   (James 3:10)

Gossip and criticism can be a problem in the church. Christians can be economical with the truth and give rise to misunderstanding. Things that are not true or are half-truth, or that are exaggerated, spread like wild fire around the church. What this does is to provide ammunition for demons to aim at those who are the subject of this gossip. Pastors and leaders are prime targets. No wonder some are experiencing breakdown in leadership as they labor under the weight of criticism and condemnation without sometimes knowing where it comes from.

The power of life and death is in the tongue (Proverbs 18:21) – churches can literally be cursed with death. This can happen when disaffected members part company over some issue. This is often done with anger and bitterness and many bad words, sometimes on both sides. So the church that is left behind and the individuals who have left can be affected by the words spoken against them. Such words as, "God is not in this church", "this work will never prosper", or, "you will never know God's blessing if you leave this church", "you are in rebellion". Many such words are spoken in anger and bitterness, and the Lord is not honored by such words.

A history of church splits
Has the church been formed out of a split? If so what were the reasons for the split and how did it occur? I know of those who have reluctantly left a church because there was no freedom in the Holy Spirit. They have done this after much heart searching and in the best possible way. In such circumstances demons will not get any advantage over the new church if those leaving have acted with integrity and been careful not to speak out of a wrong spirit. They have been led by the Holy Spirit to leave, and it is Jesus that they are seeking to obey. However, very few church splits happen like this. There are accusations of false teaching (which may be true), accusations against domination and control (which also may be true), but even when these accusations are based in truth they are often responded to in the flesh. Words of cursing will

continue to have effect until the individuals who uttered them are forgiven, blessed, and the demonic power broken (Luke 6:28).

Early and sudden death

We are all going to die one day unless we are part of the generation of believers who are alive on earth when Jesus comes again. It is not always easy to understand why some people die young. However, when a family seems frequently cursed with early deaths through disease or fatal accidents or a church suffers from loss of its leaders through early deaths, this needs investigating rather than being seen as "just one of those things".

Can Satan take life? It is clear from the Bible that in certain circumstances he can. He is described as a murderer (John 8:44). Satan was able to take the life of Job's animals, his servants and even his children (Job 1:12–15, 18–20). It is true that Satan could not attack Job and his family in this way without permission from God, because God had put a hedge of protection around all that belonged to Job (Job 1:10). This hedge was there as a result of all the acts of righteousness and prayers that Job made on behalf of himself and his family. How many Christians today have such a hedge of protection around them? There are also biblical references to Satan in connection with persecuting to death the disciples of Christ (Revelation 2:10 and 13).

Having prayed for the victims of serious accidents there is no doubt in my mind that demons can cause accidents, which for some people can end in death. Death can also come as the consequence of sickness resulting from curses. I remember praying for a man whose father and grandfather had died before their fortieth birthdays and he was thirty-nine years old! He was delivered from a curse of death and the last time I heard of him he was still alive and in his fifties.

A history of Freemasonry in the clergy or church officers

This deception affects some who are church leaders. The result of practicing Freemasonry is demonization not only for the individual and his family, but also for the office of pastor that he occupies. I remember teaching on the subject of Freemasonry at the Ellel Ministries center in Canada. On the course was the minister of a church. He told me in the coffee break that the previous minister had been a Freemason. He suspected that he needed some ministry. I agreed that I would check it out for him and asked him if he would be willing for me to pray for him in front of the rest of the course to demonstrate the consequences of stepping into an office that has been cursed. He readily agreed and I led him through some appropriate prayer after which I broke the ungodly soul tie between him and the previous minister. At this moment he fell on the floor as a spirit of Freemasonry manifested. I told the spirit of Freemasonry to leave him and after a short time he was free and regained his feet. None of us were expecting such a strong manifestation, which clearly demonstrated the relevance of what I was teaching. When a minister is appointed to the office of pastor he immediately steps into a spiritual inheritance and can be affected by any sins of the previous pastors that have not been completely dealt with in relation to their rights over that pastoral office. The incoming pastor should always pray concerning any issues arising from the past. He should thank the Lord for everything accomplished by God through the ministry of all previous church leaders from the beginning of the work, and then forgive any of their sins that have given the enemy rights to undermine him/her, or the life of the church. Specific sins may be known; if not, a general prayer can be offered. This must be followed by a prayer of deliverance where the incoming leader takes authority over all demonic powers and orders them to leave the church. The church needs to be thoroughly cleansed.

Decline in church membership
Whilst decline in church membership can stem from natural causes it should always be investigated for any spiritual causes. The enemy has been very successful in removing key Christians from their fellowship at critical times in the life of the church. A steady decline in members could possibly be the outworking of a curse against the fellowship. Sometimes lack of growth is caused by lack of willingness on the part of the leadership or church members to change. It may be that church members indicate a desire for change, but when

affected personally by the change, they resist it! In such circumstances there may be a need for personal repentance and deliverance from a spirit of fear.

Inability to experience the presence of the Lord
This is almost always associated with the activity of demons that love to rob us of this precious experience. The enemy cannot operate in a vacuum, so it is important to identify and deal with any sin in the church. The Lord may call for prayer and fasting before He reveals the specific problem that needs to be dealt with.

Inability to move in spiritual gifts
When the theology of the church is in line with Scripture and the hearts of the people are open to the Lord, there will always be an expression of God's presence and power in the life of the church. If this is not the case, then the leadership must seek the spiritual cause for this. If prayer and fasting have not changed things it is likely that deliverance will be necessary to completely deal with the problem.

Inability to keep a full-time pastor
In my opinion a pastor is essential to the life and growth of the church. If a church has difficulty in attracting or keeping a pastor there may be something radically wrong either in the history of the church or in the attitude of the current church members. Alternatively, there may be a need for a thorough spiritual cleansing of the church building.

Repeated sexual sin
There is usually a cause for this in the history of the church. The sin may either be current or in the past or both. Sexual sin gives evil spirits a foothold in the life of the church and they must be evicted by those in authority, following the repentance of those responsible. It is sometimes the case that a minister is suddenly removed without the congregation knowing why. In some cases this is because of sexual sin. The leadership can in most instances deal with the spiritual implications of this without making the sin public, unless they need to confess their own sins against the congregation.

Financial difficulties

It is not unusual for a Christian work to struggle in the area of its finances. There may be spiritual causes behind the lack of money that need investigating. It could be unwillingness on the part of believers to give to the work. Or it could be that the finances of the work are cursed, for example, by Freemasonry.

Lack of growth in established church members and no new conversions

Lack of fruit is a serious matter in the life of a believer; it indicates a lack of abiding in Jesus (John 15:4). Life produces life. As barrenness of the womb is a curse, so also is lack of conversion growth. There can be many reasons for this, and deliverance from evil spirits is only one. But if you have tried everything possible with no results then it is likely that you will need to break some demonic curses behind spiritual infertility.

Strong resistance to the healing and deliverance ministry

There are different reasons for this that in my view are all sinful. It can be wrong teaching, unbelief, fear, human control, pride, unconfessed sin, unwillingness to make Jesus Lord of the church, a stubborn heart, or an unyielding spirit. Behind all these human sins there will be a demonic power that desires to stop the church moving in deliverance. The people need to repent and drive out the demons.

Heavy spiritual atmosphere

The presence of demons always produces a heavy atmosphere. Their presence will stifle worship and make the preaching of the Word difficult for both speaker and hearer. The demons are usually attached to the negative emotions of the con-gregation, but can also be present in the church building.

Denominational pride

Pride of any kind seems to attract demons like bees to flowers. If, for example, we are convinced that our church alone is the true church, then we are in pride and demons can easily gain a foothold in the life of the church through its members. Which of us has not been guilty of the sin of pride at some time in our lives? We are called to proclaim the kingdom of God, not a particular denomination. Let us determine to build people into the kingdom of God and not our particular congregation.

Fearful and anxious church members

Fear is a chief weapon of Satan and all demons. The fear of doing something never attempted before affects many believers; it is often connected with the fear of failure. The fear of the unknown can stop believers living in the power of the Holy Spirit. There can be a fear of demonic manifestations. Experience in deliverance can help overcome this as one learns to be more effective in dealing with such manifestations. We should not fear demons because Jesus has given us His authority over them. *"Greater is He who is in you than he who is in the world"* (1 John 4:4). We cannot, however, stop all demonic manifestations. If the demons sometimes cried out when Jesus was driving them out (Mark 3:11), they are likely to do the same when we drive them out using the power that He gave to us. Why should we worry about the fear that demons experience when the power of God hits them? In the church there can be various fears that are connected to individual pain such as the fear of authority, the fear of losing control, and the negative fear of God (this is different to the holy fear of God).

Lack of freedom to speak the truth to each other in love

This may be an indication of the exercise of ungodly authority, manipulation, domination, control, and intimidation. Once they have established themselves in the life of a church they become strongholds that are not easily or quickly broken.

A feeling of hopelessness among church members

Demons love to lead believers into thinking that their circumstances are beyond remedy. A spirit of hopelessness can lie over the meeting where a number of deeply hurting people are present. It requires someone to lead the meeting or the ministry time who is overflowing with hope in the Holy Spirit (Romans 15:13).

Battling with sexual thoughts during worship
This can be caused by sexual spirits in the church building or within the individual. It can be as a consequence of sexual abuse having taken place in the building, or through such private sexual sins as pornography.

Desire to run out of church services
This can affect those who are in need of deep ministry, although the problem may be in the person and not in the building.

A fear of being in certain parts of the church building
A vicar once told me that he avoided a particular part of his church when he could, because he felt uncomfortable there. Following discussion together, we did some spiritual cleansing and the bad feeling he had experienced in this particular place disappeared.

Various plaques on the wall
It is common practice to commemorate worthy church members, normally after their death, by placing a plaque on the wall. Sometimes these individuals become idolized and are frequently pointed to as referees on any change in church practices. For example someone may say, "He wouldn't have allowed this if he were alive", or, "This will make him turn in his grave". If the individual was a practicing Freemason then the demonic power of Freemasonry could be operating behind these kinds of comments.

Chapter 9

Procedures for the Deliverance of Land, Buildings and Ministries

"The sceptre of the wicked will not remain
over the land allotted to the righteous,
for then the righteous might use
their hands to do evil."   (Psalm 125:3)

The Lord gave me this scripture some time ago when I was seeking Him before beginning the work of cleansing and delivering the land and work of the former Ellel Ministries Center in Canada. It helped me to see the desire of the Lord for His presence to be manifested, and not that of the enemy, in the land and buildings that we were occupying. The presence of the Lord is needed for a church or healing center which seeks to establish the kingdom of God in the hearts of His people. However, I knew that there was a lot of necessary preparation God needed to do in us as a team before we could begin the work. I discovered that the preparation leading up to the point of deliverance might take some time, not least in the midst of a busy ministry where there are many other things that also have to be done.

In the previous chapter we have established how to detect the presence of evil spirits, let us now consider the preparation that must be done before authority can be exercised over the demons in order to cast them out from land, buildings and ministries. First we must understand the issues of ownership and authority.

The importance of ownership

The Israelites had full authority over the Promised Land, as it had been given to them as a possession by the Lord (Leviticus 14:34; 20:24). It was their land to live in (this is still the case today) even though it belonged ultimately to God, and any land purchased that was not inherited had to go back to the original owner in the year of Jubilee (Leviticus 25:13–17). That which is owned can be dedicated to the Lord and also cleansed (Leviticus 27:22). Ownership of land and the property is an essential requirement. If the land does not belong to us we are not the one in legal authority over it and do not have the final say. However, if the owner invites others to do the job, then they can act with full authority through the co-operation of the legal owner. Legal ownership gives spiritual authority.

It is the practice today for intercessors belonging to a movement for reconciliation to visit countries, sometimes former British colonies, for the purpose of confessing the sins of their ancestors against the inhabitants of the land – who may have been forcibly removed so that white settlement could previously take place (Leviticus 26:40). Issues such as slavery and its attendant brutality and dehumanizing of men, women and children are some of the problems that are confessed, and usually forgiveness is offered from a native of the particular country whose own ancestors were the victims of such dreadful treatment. I believe that the Lord hears such prayers and the spiritual climate is likely to change as a consequence. However, it is important not to confuse this with the deliverance of the land from the demons associated with these sins. This would require full representation of the spiritual and political leaders. This leads us to the question of how far we can go or how much we can accomplish.

The extent of authority

If the spiritual and political leaders of a town, a city or a country were to come together and corporately own their personal sin as well as confessing the sins of their ancestors, this would provide all the necessary authority to render the activity of demons ineffective, and to change the spiritual atmosphere. When it comes to churches, although they are not owned personally by the pastor/vicar/minister, such leaders can act in their capacity as senior leader on behalf of the church, or can invite help from those who can minister effectively into this area. However, they themselves need to speak out the necessary confession and repentance of personal sin, confession of ancestral sin, and forgiveness to those whose sin has given the demons rights of access.

We cannot simply visit churches for the purpose of driving out any demons whose presence we discern. Even Christian leaders cannot do this in another church because they are not in authority in that church. Consequently they cannot cast out demons unless invited to do so by the appointed leader. A demonic presence in someone else's church can be bound, but only the leaders of that particular church have the authority to drive it out, especially if they let it in through their own sin!

Sin in the denominational hierarchy of a church cannot be dealt with at local level; it can only be dealt with by denominational leaders. For example, if a denominational leader ordains a homosexual minister, this will open up all the churches under that leadership to the spirit of homosexuality. In such circumstances a local church leader could protect the church he leads from the demonic power by declaring his own position that homosexuality is a sin both verbally and in writing. Of course the ramifications of such action can be enormous. But it is always costly to take a stand for the truth. A godly leader must deal with the spirit of error unless he wants to disobey the Lord. It is understood that such actions should be done in a spirit of humility.

What can a church member do in such a situation? A friend of mine, who has been a lifelong member of her denomination and served it in various capacities, has left her church over the issue of Freemasonry. The incumbent minister is a practicing Freemason and sees nothing wrong with it, whereas my friend is in a family who have felt the spiritually and physically damaging effects of this demonic deception. She tried to convince the leader of the incompatibility of Freemasonry and Christianity, but without success. Following this unfruitful discussion she decided that she could no longer receive Communion, because she knows that hands that are joined to the spirit of Freemasonry could pass on that spirit through whatever they touch. Even this did not cause the leader to reconsider his practice of Freemasonry, so she felt before the Lord that her only course of action was to leave her church, painful as that was, because she valued the truth and did not wish to give the spirit of Freemasonry any access to her life. The laying on of hands by any Christian, whether minister or bishop, can open up an individual to the spirit of Freemasonry or any other evil spirit that has been given access through this or any other occult deception.

By now you might be thinking that it is a risky business going to church. Do not be anxious, these spirits cannot visit anyone they wish. But someone with Freemasonry in their history is more vulnerable. We can ask the Lord to protect us as we stay close to Jesus. We must not let fear keep us from engaging in Christian fellowship. As we hear and obey the voice of the Lord we shall know where to worship, and whom to allow to minister to us.

Rented or hired property

When there is no ownership of the land or the building there is no authority to remove demons. However, the demons can be bound so that they cannot interfere with the occupants for the duration of the lease or hire. Binding means to tie up or to restrain, and has the effect of restricting freedom of movement or operation. Because Christian disciples have authority over demons (Luke 10:19), demons can always be bound (Matthew 12:28–29; 16:19). Although binding will restrain the activities of demons, it is not deliverance nor is it permanent. If a church meets on Sundays in a village hall or community center, it will need to bind all demons each time it meets, as they will have been given right of access through the various activities that have taken place in the hall during the week. Although this will take time, it can be added to the regular tasks of setting up the sound equipment and putting out the chairs. Binding is both a prerequisite to deliverance and something that can be done when it is not possible to do full deliverance (Matthew 16:19; 18:18–20).

Removing the rights which have given the demons access

When the presence of the demons has been discerned and their objectives exposed to the light, the work has only just begun. The question as to what sin gave the demons access must be addressed, and also who committed the sin. For example, was the sin in the founding fathers of the work, such as is often the case with Freemasonry? Has there been sin in the leadership, for example, wrong teaching, immorality etc.? In what ways were these sins dealt with, if at all? Many sins, especially those of the leader, are swept under the carpet and the leader is sent to another church, sometimes without the congregation knowing why he left the former church. Righteousness and truth have not always prevailed in the various circumstances of the life of a church. Sometimes a leader is dealt with unfairly and harshly, for example, having been removed from office because he was trying to obey the Lord! In order for the demons to be cast out, righteousness and truth must be reestablished through confession, repentance, forgiveness and a declaration of the truth where error has been proclaimed (Joshua 24:14–15).

Summary of action necessary to remove demons

- Ask the Lord for the gift of discernment to spiritually discern the demonic presence (1 Corinthians 12:10).

- Bind the strongman or ruling demon (Matthew 12:29). Note that Jesus dealt with the spirit in overall control when delivering the demonized man in the region of the Gerasenes; his name was "Legion" (Mark 5:9). Remember that demons work together in groups and usually one is in charge.

- Identify the sins that gave the demons access and then:
  - Confess the sins of the ancestors (Leviticus 26:40; Nehemiah 9:2; Psalm 106:6; Jeremiah 14:20).
  - Forgive those who sinned (Matthew 6:14; 18:21–35; Ephesians 4:32; Colossians 3:13). This is our forgiveness for the sins of others, which have affected us.
  - Bless those who have cursed the church or the land (Matthew 5:43–45; Luke 6:28).

- – Deliver the place from the spirits that came in through the particular sins.
- Repeat this process until all the demons have gone.

The enemy can have no further access to property when the owner has exercised the delegated power of the Lord Jesus to evict all demonic powers that have gained access through the sin that has been fully dealt with, unless further sin occurs.

Spiritual protection

The deliverance of people or places from demonic powers may seem a dangerous thing to do. Many Christians are frightened of demons, which is a shame, because demons are far more fearful of Christians. It is unsound thinking that reasons "If I don't bother the devil, he won't bother me". Demons will attack us anyway, but we need not be worried over an attack if we observe scriptural guidelines. No one goes to war without a little preparation, and no one in their right mind, even though they may be well trained and armed, goes to war without doing everything possible to limit injury and death by wearing the appropriate protective clothing or armor.

The armor of God

In spiritual warfare it is the spirit of man that needs protection. The Lord has of course provided exactly what we need in this respect. Turn to Ephesians 6:10–20.

Verse 10
- We need to be strong in the Lord. The strength that we need to accomplish the will of God in each situation comes out of our union with Jesus. We need to deal with anything that proves to be a hindrance to being close to the Lord and receiving His strength. This places personal healing and deliverance in the context of discipleship and effective Christian service.

Verse 11

- We need to put on the full armor of God if we are to stand against our enemy. It is easy to overcome someone if they are not fully protected. If the Lord provides us with complete protection then we must make full use of it.

Verse 12

- The opposition is not people but demonic powers. Because it appears to be people who attack us, it is natural for us to assume that they are our real enemies. Not so, according to the Scriptures. Attack through unbelievers may be expected, but it is more difficult when it comes through a fellow believer! The enemy will use everything he can to stop us from doing the will of God, including using the weaknesses of fellow Christians to undermine us in the work God has given to us. When we are in the flesh we provide an opportunity for Satan to outwit us and to work through us.

Verse 13

- When we have done everything in order to stand, we need to remain standing firm. If someone is in a strongly defended position there is not much that you can do that is effective unless you can tempt him out of his position or in some other way persuade him to come out into the open. The devil is good at waiting for an opportunity to do this very thing. So we must do everything we possibly can to stand firm in our position to hold the ground.

Verse 14

- The belt of truth. God's truth will protect us in the measure that we believe and practice it. It is not enough simply to believe in God. The demons also believe in God, although they shudder at the thought (James 2:19). We cannot expect the truth to protect us when we know that we are in disobedience. The measure that we obey the truth is the measure that we are protected. Of course there may be areas of our life unchallenged by the Lord. In these areas we can expect His protection. But if He has shown us something is wrong and we ignore Him, we are then in danger of being vulnerable to the enemy.

- The breastplate of righteousness. Godly living is essential if the breastplate of righteousness is to protect us. Jesus is our righteousness, but in order for Jesus, who is the Truth, to protect us, we must walk uprightly in all our relationships.

Verse 15

- The shoes of peace. We need to be ready for action and ready for anything. In those days not everyone wore sandals or shoes on their feet. It was essential, however, that soldiers did, so that they could be ready to move quickly. Also, among the people of God we should bring the peace of God (Isaiah 52:7) and be known as those whose lives are characterized by peace:

  "But the wisdom that comes from heaven is first of all pure; then peace-loving, considerate, submissive, full of mercy and good fruit, impartial and sincere. Peacemakers who sow in peace raise a harvest of righteousness."   (James 3:17–18)

Verse 16

- The shield of faith will help us to overcome all temptation. The large shield that the Roman soldier used was one which could protect all his vital parts. Standing on the promises of God is one way that we can use the shield, another way to use the shield is to call upon the name of Jesus when facing temptation.

Verse 17

- The helmet of salvation will protect our mind and lead us into wholeness. Another scripture describes hope as the helmet of salvation (1 Thessalonians 5:8). The head or the mind is a vulnerable part that the enemy will attack. It is fairly common to experience thoughts of defeat, or unworthiness that can lead to hopelessness or even despair. Scripture teaches that the joy of the Lord is our strength (Nehemiah 8:10). Joy is a characteristic of those who accomplish great things for God.

- We must take and use the sword of the Spirit. The Word of God will always defeat the lies of Satan and all the powers of darkness. Jesus said that truth was powerful in setting Christian disciples free (John 8:32). The best way of overcoming the lies of Satan is by the establishment of the kingdom of God within us (Luke 17:21), so that he has no foothold within us that he can use.

Verse 18

- We cannot neglect the need to pray at all times. Prayer releases the power of God and this is the power that keeps all the armor in place. God has called us not only to pray but also to act. However, to act without prayer means that we risk being out of touch with the heart of God, His will and purposes.

The use of oil and water

When seeking to cleanse and deliver buildings it is often helpful to use either oil or water for anointing furniture and stones. Pulpits, pews, organ seats, and everything wooden can be re-consecrated with anointing oil. Anything else that would be damaged by oil such as stones, fabric or wallpaper can be anointed or washed by consecrated water. Water can be prayed over just like oil.

Following prayer, the Lord will direct you in cleansing and consecrating the building. The walls of a building can be anointed from corner to corner. However, this practice should not become a technique to be followed unless directed by the Lord, nor should it be a substitute for dependence on the Holy Spirit. It is not necessary to keep your finger on the wall as you move from corner to corner. As you pray around the room, take authority over the demons exposed by the Holy Spirit and order them to leave. This can also be done outside and around the building up to the perimeter of the property. In this way the inside and outside of the building can be cleansed and delivered from evil spirits. It is necessary to invite the presence of the Lord when doing this. A foundation stone may bear the names of the founding fathers or someone else who may have been involved in occult practices such as Freemasonry. This kind of stone can be washed in the water.

Communion

The celebration of Communion in a house or a church can be a very effective means of aiding the deliverance process. Appropriate prayers for deliverance can be included in a service of Communion where the elements are consecrated. Again we must be careful not to see this as a technique. We must be led by the Lord to hold a Communion service in such circumstances. The advantages of holding Communion are that believers are strengthened spiritually and the presence of the Lord is manifested.

Praise and worship

God inhabits the praises of His people (Psalm 22:3, KJV). He draws near to us as we draw near to Him (James 4:8). The praise needs to include the name of Jesus, His victory over death, His death for sin, His resurrection from the dead, the removal of sin and guilt through His shed blood, and His worth and glory; in short the gospel. I emphasize this because there has crept into the worship of the Church what could be described as New Age songs. Let me illustrate what I mean. I was teaching in a Youth Hostel in North West Germany and the translator had not yet arrived and so someone who had never translated before kindly agreed to stand in so that the conference could begin. The sound of worship filled the conference room and then we came to the teaching. I found it difficult, although during the first session of a conference and especially the first time in another country, one can meet with some resistance. However, there had been much prayer in preparation for the conference, and the in the room immediately before it began. Yet still the translator was coming under intense heaviness, and there was no real freedom.

I asked the Lord to show me what was going on in the spiritual realm. He showed me a picture of us worshiping Him. In the center of our worship I could see angels, and they were taking our worship and directing it towards God's throne in heaven. On the outside of the congregation I could see demons, and they were taking our worship and offering it to Satan! I asked the Lord how this was possible. He drew my attention to the worship. I sensed that there was something wrong with the worship, but I couldn't think what it was. The worship team loved the Lord, I knew most of them personally, and the music was of high quality. Suddenly I became aware of the words that we had been singing, and understanding came to me. Most of them were popular worship songs currently sung in many fellowships. However, a quick mental scan of the words indicated that there was no mention of the cross or the blood of Christ. The songs included such words as river, water, rain, fire, life, and power. All these words are ambiguous and although they may be appropriate in their place, they are no substitute for the name of Jesus, and words such as the cross and resurrection.

I called the UK team together and shared this discernment with them. Their response was positive and we all felt that we had to share this with the German worship team, but were a little concerned that they may see this as a criticism. When we shared the heaviness that we all sensed and what we thought was the reason, they responded in agreement with us, which was a great relief. Furthermore, they asked if they could start the next session with some praise and worship. We all agreed, and this time the songs clearly glorified Jesus Christ and proclaimed the truth of His death and resurrection. The atmosphere changed almost immediately, and the conference proceeded with a real sense of the presence of the Lord.

The above story shows clearly the place of worship and the importance of words in worship. The presence of God comes through appropriate praise and worship; we cannot sing just any words and expect God's living presence to be among us. Also the power of the enemy decreases as the truth is proclaimed in song bringing glory to the Lord. It is important to worship the Lord in spirit and truth (John 4:23–24) as praise and thanksgiving enable us to enter God's presence to worship and open our hearts to hear Him.

Chapter 10

The Holy Presence of God

So far I have sought to teach the importance of cleansing and delivering the buildings in which we live and worship from the presence of evil spirits so that we can experience the blessed presence of God in all its fullness. We live in a world where darkness reigns throughout the land as a consequence of the sins of mankind. The living God is our Father, and our fellowship is also with the Son and the Holy Spirit (2 Corinthians 13:14; 1 John 2:23). This fellowship is described as being more wonderful than life itself (Philippians 1:21). My heart's cry is for the glory and the presence of the Spirit of God to return in all His fullness to the Church, which is the body of Christ. It is this glorious theme that I now wish to speak about.

The desire of God is to dwell with His people

The living God desires to dwell with His people, not just to visit with them. This factor marked out the Israelites as being different from all the nations of the world (1 Samuel 4:7). When the Lord commissioned Moses to build a tabernacle for Him, He said that it was so He might dwell among them:

> *"Then have them make a sanctuary for me, and I will dwell among them."* (Exodus 25:8)

Furthermore the Lord said that for this reason He brought them out of Egypt, that they might know Him and that He might dwell among them (Exodus 29:46). First though, God had to teach the people that the camp where the Israelites lived had to be holy if He was to dwell with them:

> *"Since the* LORD *your God walks in the midst of your camp to deliver you and to defeat your enemies before you, therefore your camp must be holy; and He must not see anything indecent among you lest He turn away from you."*
>
> (Deuteronomy 23:14, NASB)

There have been three places on earth where the living God has chosen to dwell. The first place was the tabernacle or tent, which He instructed Moses to build according to specific and detailed plans (Exodus 25:9).

The second place was the temple that Solomon built. Initially the idea had been his father David's (2 Samuel 7:2), but David was not allowed to build the temple because he was a man of war and had shed much blood (1 Chronicles 22:8). Solomon was a man of peace because the Lord granted Israel peace during his reign (1 Chronicles 22:9–10).

The third place of God's dwelling is in the bodies of His redeemed people. Paul tells the Corinthian believers that they must avoid all uncleanness because their bodies have become God's temple, wherein the Holy Spirit dwells (1 Corinthians 3:16; 6:18–20).

The glory of the Lord

When the tabernacle had been completed according to God's instructions, the glory of the Lord filled it and was so great that even Moses could not enter it (Exodus 40:34–38). The glory of God is described as a cloud. It was this cloud of glory that lifted from above the tabernacle when God wanted His people to break camp and set out. This cloud by day became a pillar of fire by night. It is significant to note that fire came from the presence of the Lord and consumed the very first sacrifice made in the new tabernacle (Leviticus 9:24). By this the Lord was indicating His acceptance of the tabernacle and the sacrifice. The same thing happened at the dedication of Solomon's temple. The fire of God came down from heaven following Solomon's prayer of dedication and consumed the burnt offering which was also the very first sacrifice in the newly built temple (2 Chronicles 7:1). Again we read that the glory of the Lord so filled the temple that the priests could not enter. From this we can see that associated with the presence of the Lord is the fire of God and also the glory of God.

When we come to the New Testament we see the third dwelling of God. This time it is not just among men, but actually within them! Jesus promises that the Holy Spirit who abides with them will come and dwell within them (John 14:16–17). He was referring to the outpouring of the Holy Spirit that was to take place on the day of Pentecost that is also referred to as baptism in the Holy Spirit (John 7:37–39; Acts 1:5; 2:1ff.). We see the Lord taking up His new dwelling when fire fell from heaven and settled upon each of the believers as they were all together in one place (Acts 2:1–4). And what of the glory of the Lord? Jesus is Himself the glory of the Church and as we walk in obedience to Him we reflect in some small measure His glory (Hebrews 1:3; Ephesians 3:21; 2 Corinthians 3:18).

The withdrawal of God's presence

The beautiful temple that Solomon built was destroyed by Nebuchadnezzar (2 Chronicles 36:19). This temple was rebuilt by King Herod, but it was not as glorious as Solomon's temple had been (Haggai 2:3). Even so, the disciples drew the Lord's attention to its beauty (Luke 21:5), and Jesus foretold that these stones would be thrown down, as once again God would destroy His temple on account of the sin of His people. This came to pass when in AD 70 the Roman Titus set fire to the temple (Luke 21:6). All that is left of it today is the Western Wall, sometimes called the "Wailing Wall".

For the true worshiper of the Lord, the main beauty of the House of the Lord should not be in its stones, but in the glory of the Lord (Psalm 29). The Lord cannot and will not continue to dwell amongst a rebellious and unclean people. The Israelites were warned by the Lord not to defile the land or the temple where He dwelt. Those who were unclean for whatever reason were to be put outside the camp (Numbers 5:1-4). It was important that they did not sin and bring defilement on the land as they shared the land with God Himself as a dwelling place.

> *"Do not defile the land where you live and where I dwell, for I, the* LORD, *dwell among the Israelites."* (Numbers 35:34)

When the people of God defiled the temple, the Lord had to remove the glory of His presence and He departed (Ezekiel 10 and 11). The Lord seems reluctant to leave as He withdraws His glory in three stages. This is not the end however, as in Ezekiel 43 Scripture foretells that one day a temple will be built, in which the glory of the Lord will return to His temple after the return of the Messiah and the establishment of the millennial kingdom.

> *"He said: 'Son of man, this is the place of my throne and the place for the soles of my feet. This is where I will live among the Israelites for ever. The house of Israel will never again defile my holy name – neither they nor their kings – by their prostitution and the lifeless idols of their kings at their high places. When they placed their threshold next to my threshold and their doorposts beside my doorposts, with only a wall between me and them, they defiled my holy name by their detestable practices. So I destroyed them in my anger. Now let them put away from me their prostitution and the lifeless idols of their kings, and I will live among them for ever."*
> (Ezekiel 43:7-9)

His glory and presence in the Church

Will the Lord withdraw His presence and glory from the Church as He was forced to do from the temple of Solomon? We are deceiving ourselves if we think He will not. The Jewish nation did not think that the Lord would destroy His temple, but He did (Jeremiah 7:4; 2 Kings 25:9-11). This judgement followed nearly five hundred years of neglect of God's ordinances, particularly the seventh year Sabbath of the land, which led to the captivity in Babylon. The Lord had already destroyed Shiloh where the first tabernacle was (Jeremiah 7:12). According to Scripture the Lord can remove a local church if it leaves its first love (Revelation 2:4–5).

Many churches have closed down in the twentieth century and not always because of a shift in population. Do you wish your local church to have a continuing presence in your neighborhood? The only way you can know the full blessing and presence of the Lord in your church is to recognize Jesus Christ as the only Savior given to man, for only through Jesus Christ can man find forgiveness and acceptance with the living God (Acts 4:12). Jesus must be proclaimed as Savior, Lord, Healer, Deliverer, and Baptizer in the Holy Spirit and must be worshiped as the King of kings and Lord of lords. Finally, His Word must be obeyed and taught by the leadership and the people.

The joy of God's presence

> *"You have made known to me the path of life;*
> *you will fill me with joy in your presence,*
> *with eternal pleasures at your right hand."*
>
> (Psalm 16:11)

Fellowship with God is in itself the main joy of the Christian life (Psalm 36:8). On one occasion when the Lord spoke to Abraham, He said to him, *"I am your shield and your very great reward"* (Genesis 15:1). The greatest blessing for Abraham was to know God and to have friendship with Him (2 Chronicles 20:7; James 2:23). To meet with the living God and to fellowship with Him is the most exciting and fulfilling of human activities; this is our calling (1 Corinthians 1:9). Whilst we are still on earth we cannot see Him but nonetheless we can know Him and love Him (1 Peter 1:8). One day we shall see Him face to face (Revelation 22:4; 1 Corinthians 13:12). The apostle Paul enjoyed such wonderful close fellowship with the Lord that he could say:

> *"For to me, living is for Christ, and dying is even better. Yet if I live that means fruitful service for Christ. I really don't know which is better. I'm torn between two desires: Sometimes I*

want to live, and sometimes I long to go and be with Christ.
That would be far better for me, but it is better for you that I
live."　　　　　　　　　　　　(Philippians 1:21–24, NLT)

In conclusion

There is a popular worship song that we sing today that speaks of the days in which we live as being like the days of Moses and Elijah. I believe it is more correct to say that these days are like the days of Nehemiah. The walls are broken down and the gates have been destroyed by fire (Nehemiah 1:3). A city's walls were its defense against the enemy.

Because of childhood rejection and wrong choices, often leading to a sinful lifestyle, many Christians are living with broken walls in their own lives. Therefore, since the Church is made up of individuals, many churches have broken walls, and the enemy is able to get in and to attack and destroy. For too long we have allowed this to happen. Now is the time for church leaders to rise up and to close the gaps by repairing the spiritual walls. If we don't do it whilst we still have the day, we shall not be able to do it at all as we shall be overtaken by the darkness that is coming (John 9:4). The task will not be easy. However, the devil's tactics remain the same as they were in the days of Nehemiah:

- Ridicule from those who pretended to be friends (Nehemiah 2:19)
- Anger from the enemies of God (Nehemiah 4:1)
- False accusation (Nehemiah 2:19; 6:5–8)
- Discouragement: "The task is too great for you, even if you succeed it will not last" (Nehemiah 4:2–3)
- Distractions (Nehemiah 6:2–4)
- Death threats (Nehemiah 6:10–13)

Nehemiah overcame all this opposition by applying himself to the task, by refusing to give in to intimidation and fear for his own life. He overcame through God-given strategy in prayer and spiritual warfare (Nehemiah 4:19–23). He and his workers completed the task in a staggering fifty-two days (Nehemiah 6:15). Note that Scripture records that this caused the enemies of God to become fearful and to lose their self-confidence (Nehemiah 6:16). We can keep going because in reality the enemy is already defeated at the cross. All his tactics are fruitless if we persist in the will of God, for he cannot defeat the will and purposes of Almighty God.

> *"Our Father in heaven,*
> *hallowed be your name,*
> *your kingdom come,*
> *your will be done*
> *   on earth as it is in heaven."*   (Matthew 6:9–10)

The last days

The Day of Judgement is coming when the Lord will not only judge men and women who have rejected His Son, Jesus, but when He will also judge the powers of the air. They are responsible for so much death and destruction of human life and they have spread darkness and uncleanness over the face of the earth. For this they will have to suffer the consequences of their rebellion against their Lord and Creator.

> *"In that day the* Lord *will punish*
> *   the powers in the heavens above*
> *   and the kings on the earth below.*
> *They will be herded together*
> *   like prisoners bound in a dungeon;*
> *they will be shut up in prison*
> *   and be punished after many days."*   (Isaiah 24:21–22)

Following the great tribulation, the Lord will cleanse the earth through fire from all its defilement in preparation for His millennial reign:

> *"See, the* Lord *is going to lay waste the earth*
> *   and devastate it;*
> *he will ruin its face*
> *   and scatter its inhabitants . . .*

The earth will be completely laid waste
and totally plundered.
The LORD has spoken this word ...

The earth is defiled by its people;
they have disobeyed the laws,
violated the statutes
and broken the everlasting covenant.
Therefore a curse consumes the earth;
its people must bear their guilt.
Therefore earth's inhabitants are burned up,
and very few are left ...
The moon will be abashed, the sun ashamed;
for the LORD Almighty will reign
on Mount Zion and in Jerusalem,
and before its elders, gloriously."

(Isaiah 24:1, 3, 5–6, 23)

The Lord will also restore the fortunes of Israel and will gather the nations of the world together in the valley of Jehoshaphat, where He will judge them for their hatred and rejection of Israel and their dividing of the land of Israel:

"For behold, in those days and at that time,
When I restore the fortunes of Judah and Jerusalem,
I will gather all the nations
And bring them down to the valley of Jehoshaphat.
Then I will enter into judgment with them there
On behalf of My people and My inheritance, Israel,
Whom they have scattered among the nations;
And they have divided up My land."   (Joel 3:1–2, NASB)

Satan's man, the Antichrist, who will appear so powerful through his mighty reign as the world leader (Revelation 13:8) will be stripped of all his powers and become as weak as other world leaders who will be surprised to see him so weak and powerless:

"The grave below is all astir
to meet you at your coming;

> *it rouses the spirits of the departed to greet you –*
>   *all those who were leaders in the world;*
> *it makes them rise from their thrones –*
>   *all those who were kings over the nations.*
> *They will all respond,*
>   *they will say to you,*
> *"You also have become weak, as we are;*
>   *you have become like us."*   (Isaiah 14:9–10)

And the day is coming when Satan will be thrown into the lake of burning sulfur with the beast and the false prophet.

> *"When the thousand years are over, Satan will be released from his prison and will go out to deceive the nations in the four corners of the earth – Gog and Magog – to gather them for battle. In number they are like the sand on the seashore. They marched across the breadth of the earth and surrounded the camp of God's people, the city he loves. But fire came down from heaven and devoured them. And the devil, who deceived them, was thrown into the lake of burning sulphur, where the beast and the false prophet had been thrown. They will be tormented day and night for ever and ever."*
>   (Revelation 20:7–10)

The new heavens and the new earth

Following the final rebellion spoken of in Revelation 20:7–9, earth and heaven will become one and the glory of God's presence will fill the earth *"as the waters cover the sea"* (Habakkuk 2:14):

> *"Then I saw a new heaven and a new earth, for the first heaven and the first earth had passed away, and there was no longer any sea. I saw the Holy City, the new Jerusalem, coming down out of heaven from God, prepared as a bride beautifully dressed for her husband. And I heard a loud voice from the throne saying, 'Now the dwelling of God is with men, and he will live with them. They will be his people, and God himself will be with them and be their God. He will wipe every tear from their eyes. There will be no more death or mourning or*

crying or pain, for the old order of things has passed away.' He who was seated on the throne said, 'I am making everything new!' Then he said, 'Write this down, for these words are trustworthy and true.' He said to me: 'It is done. I am the Alpha and the Omega, the Beginning and the End. To him who is thirsty I will give to drink without cost from the spring of the water of life. He who overcomes will inherit all this, and I will be his God and he will be my son.'"

(Revelation 21:1–7)

Jesus said, *"Yes I am coming soon."* The heart's cry of God's children is *"Amen. Come, Lord Jesus. The grace of the Lord Jesus be with God's people. Amen"* (Revelation 22:20–21).

Appendix

Sample Prayers

Lordship prayer

This prayer is for a church that has already been dedicated to the worship of the Lord. It is important that the leadership declare their desire for the church that they lead to be submitted to the Lordship of Jesus. The following prayers are model prayers that can be adapted as appropriate.

> We declare before God and the whole company of heaven and earth that we desire that this church (name specific church or ministry) be submitted to and directed by Jesus Christ of Nazareth who is Lord of the universal Church, which is His body. We declare to Satan and all the powers of darkness in the name of Jesus Christ the Lord that you have no place in this church or on the ground upon which this church is built. We declare that it is my/our intention that as truth and light from the Lord exposes you and all your works, we will drive you and all your demons from this church/ministry.

Prayers of repentance

> Lord, we confess that we have sinned against you in thought, word and deed. We confess our sins of (be specific here) and ask that you would forgive us and deliver the church and the people of this church from any consequences of our sins. We confess that we have not strengthened the weak, or healed the sick, neither

have we bound up the injured. We have not brought back the strays or searched for the lost. We have ruled them brutally and harshly. Please forgive us, cleanse us from all our sin, and grant that from this day forward we may express your heart of love for your people, and lead them gently in the ways of truth and righteousness.

General forgiveness prayer for those who have cursed the church and its people

We forgive every person, Christian or non-Christian, who has directly or indirectly cursed this church/minister/ministry, through their words or their actions. We break the power of every curse that Satan has put upon this church/minister/ministry. We specifically break the power of (here you may need to mention sickness, marital breakdown or something else that you know Satan has afflicted the church with) every curse affecting this church/minister/ministry and we command every evil spirit to go in the mighty name of Jesus Christ of Nazareth. We ask, Lord, that you would destroy every weapon that the enemy has forged against us.

Prayer for release from Satanic and witchcraft curses

Father, we come in the name of Jesus Christ of Nazareth asking that you would release us from every demon that has been assigned to this person/church/ministry through any Satanic or witchcraft ritual. We forgive all those who are opposed to the kingdom of God and we release them into the freedom of my/our forgiveness. We now break every spirit of curse affecting this church/ministry/person and ask that you would send your angels to destroy any picture or any personal belonging that has been used in specific satanic or witchcraft rituals.

Prayer for the sins of previous church leaders

This is a prayer for the senior pastor/minister to offer, although it can be said by a church leadership where there is no resident pastor/minister.

We come before the Lord to confess the sins of all previous church leaders (mention specific leaders where particular sins are known). We thank you for all the truth and blessings that have come from you through every leader in this church since it began. We confess all the sins of every church leader (mention here the name of the church) since the work began. We confess the sins of (mention specific leaders that are known to have sinned) and we renounce all their sins (mention specific sins where they are known). I/We forgive them for all their sins that have affected us as the present leadership and ask that you would deliver us and the church from all the consequences of their sins known and unknown.

Prayer for deliverance from demons

We now take authority over every demon that has gained a foothold in this church through the sins of (mention specific sins) which have been repented of and renounced. We break every ungodly soul tie between us and every previous leader (mention specific leaders) and ask that you would separate us and this church from their sins. We now command every demon of (mention specific sins) to leave this church and never return. We break your power over this work and off every person connected with this church.

Prayer for the dedication and consecration of a new building for Christian worship

We dedicate and consecrate the land upon which this church is built and the building itself, to the glory of God the Father, the Son, and the Holy Spirit. We now set it apart for the praise and worship of the living God, the proclamation of the gospel of Jesus Christ, the eternally begotten Son of God, and the celebration of the sacraments of Holy Communion and Baptism. It is our intention that only that which is pleasing to the Lord should be allowed within these hallowed walls and grounds, and we will do the utmost within our power to fulfil this declaration and our sacred responsibility. We ask that all who minister in the name of the Lord in this place of worship will be anointed by the Holy Spirit and protected by the Lord. We now take authority over every evil spirit (you will need to be specific here) in the name of Jesus Christ of Nazareth who came in the flesh, and command you to depart forever from the ground upon which this church is built. We break every curse and order the spirits of curse to depart from this building and these grounds. We invite the Lord of lords to send His Holy Spirit to cleanse this ground and building and to dwell over it and within its walls (oil or water may be used to anoint the walls and furniture as directed by the Holy Spirit).

Dedication of a home

Dear Lord Jesus, we thank you for providing this new house for us to live in. We pray that it will be a safe and pleasant home for us and all who enter within its walls. We forgive any sin that has occurred on the ground upon which the house is built, and any opening that this has given to the powers of darkness (be specific here, if research or revelation from the Lord has indicated specific sins). We forgive all those who have previously lived here for anything that they have done that has given access to evil spirits (again, be specific here, if research or revelation from the Lord has indicated specific sins). We now dedicate this house, the land upon which our house is built, and everything within it in the name of Father, Son and Holy Spirit. May nothing evil be allowed within these walls but only that which is pleasing to the Lord. We now take authority in the name of Jesus Christ of Nazareth over every evil spirit and order it to leave our property now and never return. We break every curse and order the spirits of curse to depart from this building and these grounds. (Again, oil or water may be used to anoint the walls as directed by the Holy Spirit.)

Prayer for the blessing of oil

Father, we thank you for this oil that you have created, and we bless this oil in the name of Jesus Christ the Lord and ask that you would sanctify it to the consecration and cleansing of this ground/church/ministry/furniture by sending your Holy Spirit to make it holy. We take authority over every evil spirit on this ground, in this church or ministry, and we command you to go in the mighty name of Jesus Christ of Nazareth.

Prayer for the blessing of water

Father, we thank you for this water that you have created and we bless this water in the name of Jesus Christ the Lord and ask that you would sanctify it to the consecration and cleansing of this stone/carpet/curtains. We take authority over every evil spirit attached to these articles and we command you to go in the mighty name of Jesus Christ of Nazareth.

We hope you enjoyed reading this Sovereign World book.
For more details of other Sovereign books and
new releases see our website:

www.sovereignworld.com

If you would like to help us send a copy of this book
and many other titles to needy pastors in the Third World,
please write for further information or send your gift to:

Sovereign World Trust
PO Box 777
Tonbridge, Kent TN11 0ZS
United Kingdom

You can also visit **www.sovereignworldtrust.com**.
The Trust is a registered charity.